TECH, SPEC & GRADE A BRA & BRIEF

When I entered my first job I was surprised how little I knew about the technical side of lingerie. Previously I had just completed three years at University and a work placement, yet I only had the basic knowledge of grading, couldn't read a spec sheet and had not written a tech pack before. I then worked for a UK lingerie manufacturer where luckily I got to follow the design process from start to finish.

After writing my first book "How to become a lingerie designer.' I realised there was a gap in knowledge base for the technical side of designing lingerie and led to my writing of this book.

The same styles of lingerie are used throughout the chapters How to Spec a Bra & Brief, How to write a Tech Pack and How to Grade a Bra & Brief so you can follow the process.

By learning the technical side of lingerie design it will make the minefield that is going it alone, starting up or improving your knowledge base that much easier.

This knowledge will make it easier to source and communicate with factories and understand all the procedures it takes to bring your ideas to fruition.

all the best...

LvJ

CHAPTER 1

HOW TO
WRITE A
BRA
& BRIEF
PACK

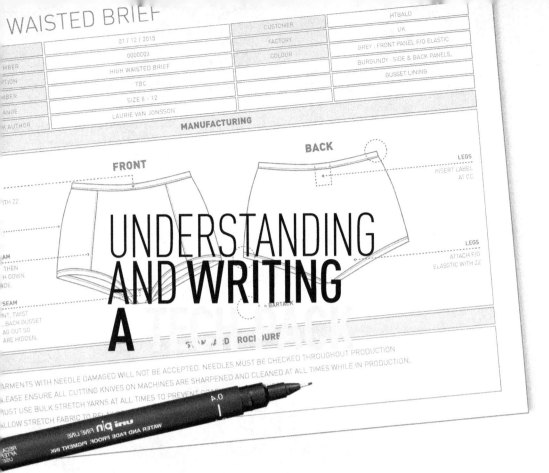

UNDERSTANDING AND WRITING A TECH PACK

Learning how to write a tech pack is the gateway for your designs to become a reality.

This booklet provides how to lay out a tech pack, and all the information that you need in it. It will also give you some of the sewing terms used in the lingerie industry; so right from the start your Tech Pack will look professional.

A tech pack is a vital piece in manufacturing transforming the idea from your head and passing it forwards to form the exact garment you want. It stops frustration from both parties as all the information is laid out clearly and precise for everyone.

To keep it simple, the book gets straight to the point, and although different companies use different layouts I've kept in the basic information so you can concentrate on getting the information correct.

By the end of this booklet you will be able to put together your own tech pack. Start by looking at garments and see how they are constructed; as this will assist you when you're trying to construct your own tech pack.

WHAT IS A PACK?

A tech pack contains all the instructions a factory needs to create a design. The designer or possibly a technician that has worked closely with them usually prepares it.

It is the main tool to give a designer the chance to work out and prepare in detail the design of their garment. It will include the trims, the finishes, the proportions, the appearance and the color placement, etc. By having a tech pack it gives you the designer, the chance to flush out any mistakes before production. The more information about the specific finish of your garment the better your prototype or production sample will turn out.

Tech pack formats can vary between manufacturer, and the details given in a tech pack are likely to vary depending on the size of the company.

The purpose of a tech pack is so the production department can go ahead with manufacturing without having to refer back to the designer on each aspect of production. The bigger the company, the more detailed a tech pack usually is, for the simple reason that it'll pass through many hands before it reaches production. It needs to be accurately exact in line with want the designer wants, and what the buyer has signed off, otherwise it will result in a huge production loss.

A tech pack can be used to manage and co-ordinate the various activities in the production line. A well-presented tech pack will bring efficiency within a company, as various departments can refer back, seeking the answers they may need.

Think of manufacturing as putting a puzzle together; you are presenting different shapes, sizes and colours, and by providing the instructions (a tech pack) it can be produced exactly like the reference sample and to the correct specification.

KEEPING A PRODUCTION FILE

Before we discuss what goes in a Tech Pack, you need to understand what a Tech Pack isn't. What it isn't; is a production pack. A production pack is information you've been gathering as your design has been going along. This information is usually kept in a production file. This would include information such as fabric testing, approved colours etc.

The person, who keeps a production file, will differ on the company size. Sometimes it'll be an actual production team member, in others it'll be the designer. Your production file will be built as the design goes along, it'll contain all the required information that you need as a reference for that garment. Any questions arising about this style should be able to be found in here.

> Keeping all the information in a simple A4 folder will do the trick.

If you are an independent designer, your production file will contain far less pages, as you the designer will have full control over the every decision and design, and won't have to consult the buyer to sign anything off.

The production file (depending on the size of the company) should contain the following.

Production File Checklist

- 1. Production Order sheet ☐
- 2. Comment sheet ☐
- 3. PP Meeting sheet ☐
- 4. Approved Fabric Swatch sheet ☐
- 5. Approved Strike Off sheet ☐
- 6. Trim Card sheet ☐
- 7. Label Approval sheet ☐
- 8. FPT/GPT Report sheet ☐
- 9. PP Size Set Sample sheet ☐
- 10. Shipment Sample sheet ☐

1_Production Order Sheet
This is the order sheet from the buyer; it'll be have the name, the style number, colour of the garment and a size break down. It will also have the unit price of the garment and the total amount. Terms and conditions and payment details can also be outlined at the bottom as well.

2_Comment Sheet
This is any comments/emails that have come from the buyer regarding this style. This can be from, delivery times or changes of the style etc.

3_PP Meeting Sheet
These are the garments fitting comments from your Pre-Production sample. There should be a copy of an approved Pre-Production sample spec sheet, signed and dated by the buyer. These comments can be in diagram form, written on the spec sheet, for which measurements need to change.

4_Approved Fabric Swatches
This is will a card with every approved fabric you are using on the garment. This could be approved by the buyer or chosen by you the designer. This also includes any lab dips that you have had done.

5_Approved Strike Offs
Strike-Off approval is what is given if you have designed a print to go on fabric. You will be checking for colour, design and if it's a repeat pattern then a larger sample will be sent to you to make sure the repeat can be approved.

6_Trim Card
This will be an approved list and swatches of all your components that you are using of your garment. Eg buttons, lace, elastic etc.

7_Label Approval
This will be the artwork for the label, and then the actual printed label. Including swing tickets, care label, brand label and price tickets. This is may not be included if you are a small company, you may be using the same label throughout all designs.

8_FPT/GPT Report
A Fabric Package/Performance Test (FPT) or a Garment Package/Performance Test (GPT) are the tests in which fabric under goes, to meet your (or the buyers) standards. These requirements will vary based on the fabric type etc. This could be colour fastening after 'x' amounts of washes, appearance after laundering, seam strength etc. If all requested test results don't meet or exceed buyer specified requirement then the fabric is not approved; fabric will be sent for re-processing. Tests will be fewer in GPT as most of the performance tests are covered in FPT.

9_PP Size Set Sample Sheet
Before your production samples are made, Pre-Production (PP) size set samples are manufactured. These are to check that every size fits together and to catch any problems that might occur before production. These garments don't have to be in the correct bulk fabric but are advised to be as close as possible due to measurements. Once received they are cross referenced and checked against the spec sheet for measurements and checked against the Tech pack for construction.

10_Shipment Sample Sheet
Once production is underway, one full size set of Shipping Samples (taken from production) is checked and sent onto the buyer (if needing buyers approval).

At the start of the folder, place the checklist, so at one glance you can see what has been approved and what you are waiting for. The checklist should have a time line with the start of production to ex-factory date (when the goods leave the factory). This will ensure you're on track.

WHAT SHOULD I PUT IN A TECH PACK?

The Tech Pack contains all of the instructions that a factory will require to create the garment from start to finish.

At basic it will contain:
- A technical sketch of the garment, front and back with close-ups of unusual details
- All construction and sewing details
- A list of fabrics, trims and components, including suppliers if available
- Any artwork for prints, patterns, labels etc.
- Packing and shipping instructions

A Tech pack usually has each detail of information on separate pages, so you're likely to see:

Checklist
- [ ] Summary page
- [ ] Construction page
- [ ] Fabric and Component page
- [ ] Specification Sheet
- [ ] Label page
- [ ] Packing and Shipping page

_1. A summary page

This will have the garment style number, date of production, delivery date, and a drawn picture of garment (usually using Adobe Illustrator).

A checklist of what has and needs to be done, ie sample garment sent, fabric sent, any artwork approved.

SUMMARY PAGE — TECH PACK

DATE		CUSTOMER	
STYLE NUMBER		FACTORY	
DESCRIPTION		COLOUR	
PO NUMBER			
SIZE RANGE			
TECH PACK AUTHOR			

PRODUCTION

CHECKLIST			IMAGE
ITEM	DONE	COMMENT	
FABRIC CHOSEN			
COLOUR SWATCHES			
ARTWORK			
TRIMS APPROVED			
SIZE SPEC			
PACKAGING			
PATTERNS			
SAMPLE APPROVED			
PP SAMPLE			
SHIPPING SAMPLES			

DELIVERY DATE / /

IMPORTANT INFORMATION

_2. Construction page

This will be a front and back technical sketch with in-depth details of how the garment is constructed. Also written would be any important information that goes against the usual make-up of the garment. The example shows the information that would be noted on a construction page.

If you have different colours of fabrics and trims on your lingerie, you may want to do a separate page, stating each colour part of the lingerie.

BRIEF — TECH PACK

DATE	
STYLE NUMBER	
DESCRIPTION	
PO NUMBER	
SIZE RANGE	
TECH PACK AUTHOR	

CUSTOMER	
FACTORY	
COLOUR	

MANUFACTURING BRIEF

- WAIST
- SIDESEAMS
- GUSSET SEAM

FRONT   BACK

- LABEL
- LEGS
- BOWS

◯ = BARTACK

STANDARD PROCEDURES

1.
2.
3.
4.

BRA Front

TECH PACK

DATE		CUSTOMER	
STYLE NUMBER		FACTORY	
DESCRIPTION		COLOUR	
PO NUMBER			
SIZE RANGE			
TECH PACK AUTHOR			

MANUFACTURING FRONT OF BRA

- STRAPS
- CUP
- STRAPS
- CUP

◯ = BARTACK

STANDARD PROCEDURES

1.
2.
3.
4.

BRA Back

TECH PACK

DATE		CUSTOMER	
STYLE NUMBER		FACTORY	
DESCRIPTION		COLOUR	
PO NUMBER			
SIZE RANGE			
TECH PACK AUTHOR			

MANUFACTURING BACK OF BRA

- UNDERWIRE
- TOP WING
- SIDE BONING
- CARE LABEL
- STRAPS
- HOOK AND EYE
- UNDERBAND

◯ = BARTACK

STANDARD PROCEDURES

1.
2.
3.
4.

_3. Fabric and component page

This sheet should list all of the fabrics, components and trims used in the manufacture of the garment, including fabric references and supplier if the information is available. Even if you use the same under-wire casing for every garment, still put in the supplier code. There is nothing more frustrating than following a style, which states 'as per previous style number'. Where it states 'sourcing guidelines' an example of what to put in here would be if you wanted your galloon lace to be of a certain width, or you wanted your edge elastic to have a certain edge.

BRIEF TRIMS — TECH PACK

DATE		CUSTOMER	
STYLE NUMBER		FACTORY	
DESCRIPTION		COLOUR	
PO NUMBER			
SIZE RANGE			
TECH PACK AUTHOR			

TRIMS

LACE	ELASTIC	BOWS
ARTICLE NUMBER: COMPOSITION: PLACEMENT: SOURCING GUIDELINES -	ARTICLE NUMBER: COMPOSITION: PLACEMENT: SOURCING GUIDELINES -	ARTICLE NUMBER: COMPOSITION: PLACEMENT: SOURCING GUIDELINES -
RINGS	**SLIDES**	**HOOK AND EYES**
ARTICLE NUMBER: COMPOSITION: PLACEMENT: SOURCING GUIDELINES -	ARTICLE NUMBER: COMPOSITION: PLACEMENT: SOURCING GUIDELINES -	ARTICLE NUMBER: COMPOSITION: PLACEMENT: SOURCING GUIDELINES -

STANDARD PROCEDURES

BRA TRIMS

TECH PACK

DATE		CUSTOMER	
STYLE NUMBER		FACTORY	
DESCRIPTION		COLOUR	
PO NUMBER			
SIZE RANGE			
TECH PACK AUTHOR			

TRIMS

BRA STRAPPING	BRUSH BACK ELASTIC	PLASTIC BONING
ARTICLE NUMBER: PLACEMENT: SIDE SEAMS:	ARTICLE NUMBER: PLACEMENT: SIDE SEAMS:	ARTICLE NUMBER: PLACEMENT: SIDE SEAMS:
CUPS	**UNDERWIRE**	**11MM WIRE CASING**
ARTICLE NUMBER: COMPOSITION: PLACEMENT:	ARTICLE NUMBER: COMPOSITION: PLACEMENT:	ARTICLE NUMBER: COMPOSITION: PLACEMENT:
RINGS	**SLIDES**	**HOOK AND EYES**
ARTICLE NUMBER: PLACEMENT:	ARTICLE NUMBER: PLACEMENT:	ARTICLE NUMBER: COMPOSITION: PLACEMENT:

STANDARD PROCEDURES

_4. Specification sheet

A full spec of every size garment you want to manufacture, and a breakdown of quantity, remember to have it signed and dated when the garment was approved for fit. This confirms that this is the correct spec. For a more detailed look into how a Spec Sheet is put together. The booklet "How to spec a bra and brief" is available.

SIZE SPECIFICATION			STYLE NO: 001		SUPPLIER: HOW TO BECOME A LINGERIE DESIGNER			
GARMENT DESCRIPTION:		Basic Brief						
REF	POINT OF MEASUREMENT		XS	S	M	L		TOL (-)
A	1/2 waist relaxed		23.4	25.9	28.4	30.9		0.5
B	1/2 waist stretched		38.0	40.5	43.0	45.5		1
C	Front rise		9.0	10.0	11.0	12.0		0.5
D	Back rise		15.5	16.5	17.5	18.5		0.5
E	Gusset length		10.7	10.7	10.7	10.7		0.5
F	Front gusset width		5.5	6.0	6.0	6.0		0.5
G	Gusset at narrowest point		4.5	5.0	5.0	5.0		0.5
H	Back gusset width		6.7	7.2	7.2	7.2		0.5
I	1/2 leg relaxed		20.7	22.1	23.5	24.9		0.5
J	1/2 leg stretched		32.2	33.6	35.0	36.4		1
K	Side seam length		9.8	10.3	10.3	10.3		0.5

Special Instructions:

NAME: LVJ   DATE: 01/12/2014

_5. Label page

An illustration and description of tags/labels used on the garment. Where the label is placed and how it is attached. Including the swing ticket, fabric brand label, washing label, and any stickers. For smaller independent brands, doing a small run, there are pre-made labels available, with washing instructions pre applied.

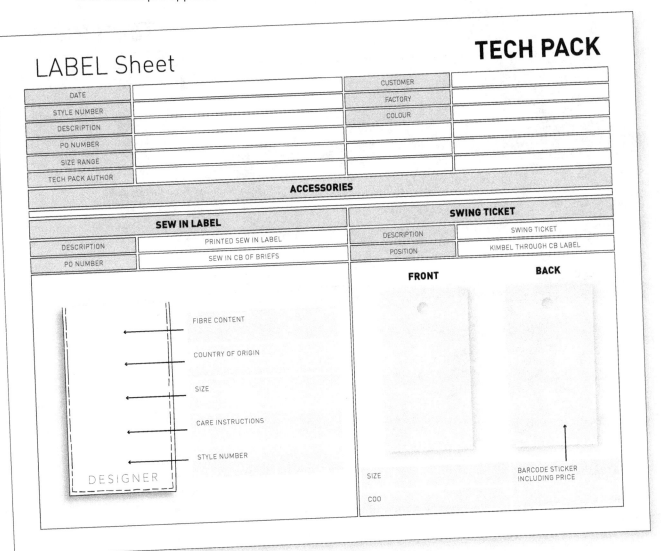

_6. Packing and Shipping

The manner in which you want the product packed, all in one box/x-amount in one box etc. Also how you want the items shipped.

PACKING Sheet

TECH PACK

DATE		CUSTOMER	
STYLE NUMBER		FACTORY	
DESCRIPTION		COLOUR	
PO NUMBER			
SIZE RANGE			
TECH PACK AUTHOR			

ACCESSORIES

PACKING QUANTITIES	RATIO PACK BREAK DOWN
PLEASE PACK THE GARMENTS IN THE FOLLOWING QUANTITIES	SIZE / TOTAL

EXTRA INFORATION

INCOTERMS

If you deal with any overseas factories then you will have to learn and state shipment in what is called Incoterms.

"The Incoterms rules or International Commercial Terms are a series of pre-defined commercial terms published by the International Chamber of Commerce (ICC) that are widely used in International commercial transactions or Procurement processes. A series of three-letter trade terms related to common contractual sales practices, the Incoterms rules are intended primarily to clearly communicate the tasks, costs, and risks associated with the transportation and delivery of goods. The Incoterms rules are accepted by governments, legal authorities, and practitioners worldwide for the interpretation of most commonly used terms in international trade. They are intended to reduce or remove altogether uncertainties arising from different interpretation of the rules in different countries. As such they are regularly incorporated into sales contracts worldwide".

INCOTERMS - CHARTS OF REPONSIBILITY

CHARGES / FEES	ANY TRANSPORT MODE		SEA / INLAND WATERWAY TRANSPORT				ANY TRANSPORT MODE				
	EXW	FCA	FAS	FOB	CFR	CIF	CPT	CIP	DAT	DAP	DDP
	EX WORKS	FREE CARRIER	FREE ALONGSIDE SHIP	FREE ON BOARD	COST & FREIGHT	COST INSURANCE & FREIGHT	CARRIAGE PAID TO	CARRIAGE INSURANCE PAID TO	DELIVERY AT TERMINAL	DELIVERY AT PLACE	DELIVERED DUTY PAID
PACKAGING	BUYER	SELLER	SELLER	SELLER	SELLER	SELLER	SELLER	SELLER	SELLER	SELLER	SELLER
LOADING CHARGES	BUYER	SELLER	SELLER	SELLER	SELLER	SELLER	SELLER	SELLER	SELLER	SELLER	SELLER
DELIVERY TO PORT	BUYER	SELLER	SELLER	SELLER	SELLER	SELLER	SELLER	SELLER	SELLER	SELLER	SELLER
EXPORT DUTY & TAX	BUYER	SELLER	SELLER	SELLER	SELLER	SELLER	SELLER	SELLER	SELLER	SELLER	SELLER
ORIGIN TERMINAL CHARGES	BUYER	BUYER	SELLER	SELLER	SELLER	SELLER	SELLER	SELLER	SELLER	SELLER	SELLER
LOADING ON CARRIAGE	BUYER	BUYER	BUYER	SELLER	SELLER	SELLER	SELLER	SELLER	SELLER	SELLER	SELLER
CARRIAGE CHARGES	BUYER	BUYER	BUYER	BUYER	SELLER	SELLER	SELLER	SELLER	SELLER	SELLER	SELLER
INSURANCE	-	-	-	-	-	SELLER	-	SELLER	-	-	-
DESTINATION TERMINAL CHARGES	BUYER	BUYER	BUYER	BUYER	BUYER	BUYER	SELLER	SELLER	SELLER	SELLER	SELLER
DELIVERY TO DESTINATION	BUYER	BUYER	BUYER	BUYER	BUYER	BUYER	BUYER	BUYER	BUYER	SELLER	SELLER
IMPORT DUTY & TAXES	BUYER	BUYER	BUYER	BUYER	BUYER	BUYER	BUYER	BUYER	BUYER	BUYER	SELLER

* CORRECT AS OF 2015

Source: en.wikipedia.org/wiki/Incoterms

Basically each term is an abbreviation of three letters long, to determine who pays for shipment and who is responsible for the goods when and where in transit and the cover of import duties.

_7. Cost page

This page is not always added, it depends on whether the factory is sourcing and ordering your fabrics. If you did include this page it would include the amounts of fabrics needed to complete the order and the amounts of trims and components needed.

CONSTRUCTION TECH PAGE AND SEWING TERMS

When putting together a Tech Pack for the first time, some people struggle with the construction page. On this page you will need every sewing procedure that goes into making your garment.

Where to start?
If you have no idea where to start I would recommend looking at the lingerie you already own and work backwards at creating a construction page for the lingerie you are looking at. This would include, the overlocking of the side seams, how the elastic is attached, any bows, and bar-tacking etc (see example of construction page provided).

As well as writing the sewing procedures you will need to know the abbreviations; the extent and detail of your garment will dictate how much space there is to write the sewing operations.

Before we look at the layout of the tech pack construction page, let's look at a few sewing terms. Please be aware some companies may use different sewing terms when discussing these techniques.

Bartack
A group of closely sewn stitching (sewn back and forth from side to side with a zigzag stitch).

Butting
Two edges of fabrics together but not overlapping, joined usually by zigzagging the edges together.

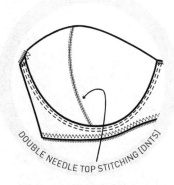

Double Needle Top Stitching (DNTS)
Two parallel needles creating two lines of stitching over the fabric or seam.

Edge Stitch
A stitch done approx. 1/8" from the edge or seam.

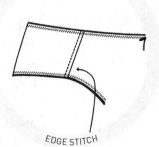

Flat Felled Seam
A seam created by sewing fabric wrong sides together, trimming one of the seam allowances close to the seam, then turning the other seam allowance under and top stitching it over the prior trimmed seam allowance. Used for reinforcing seams on pyjamas or to reduce bulk in a seam.

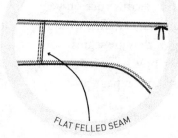

Fluted Overlock
Usually a serged (overlocked) edge that has been stretched as it has been sewn. This results in a wavey edge on the finished garment.

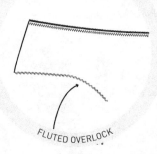

Zig Zag (Z/Z)
A stitch that goes one way (zig) and then the other (zag), can be used to attach elastic to the garment.

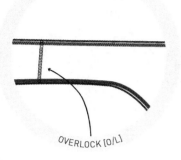

Overlock (O/L)
A type of sewing machine that stitches the seam, encases the seam with thread, and cuts off excess fabric at the same time. These are used to finish seams of any fabric, especially those that might unravel. Sometimes referred to as a Serger.

Pintuck
Narrow sewn rows of fabric that give a decorative raised look to a garment.

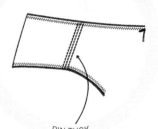

Rouching
Gathering the fabric, usually along a seam, to provide decoration.

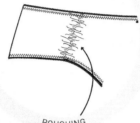

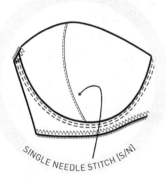

Single Needle Stitch (S/N)
A straight stitch (this is a regular stitch).

Two Needle Stitch (2N)
Parallel straight stitches, usually used to go round the wire casing.

Top Stitch
A single needle decorative and sometimes functional; it is usually 1/4" from the edge of a seam.

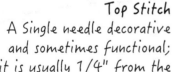

3-Step
A stitch which forms a zig-zag, but for every zig or zag it has three straight running stitches. Used to attach elastics, so the garment can stretch on the body when worn.

CONSTRUCTION
PAGE EXAMPLES

On the following pages are examples of construction pages using different shaped briefs and bras. Each of these styles can be found in the book 'How to Spec a bra and brief', along with their Specification Sheets

(Examples of the full tech pack for a darted bra and basic brief can be found later in this book).

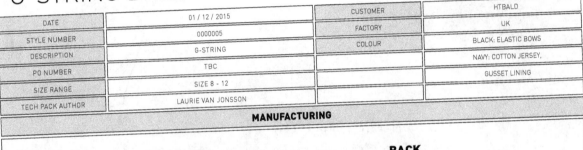

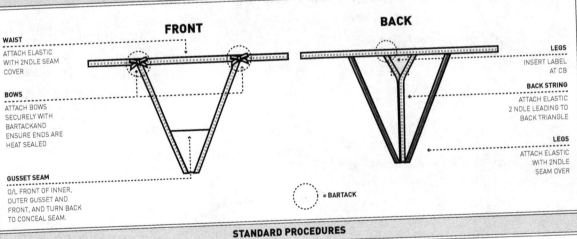

HIGH WAISTED BRIEF

TECH PACK

DATE	01 / 12 / 2015	CUSTOMER		HTBALD
STYLE NUMBER	0000003	FACTORY		UK
DESCRIPTION	HIGH WAISTED BRIEF	COLOUR		GREY : FRONT PANEL F/O ELASTIC
PO NUMBER	TBC			BURGUNDY : SIDE & BACK PANELS,
SIZE RANGE	SIZE 8 - 12			GUSSET LINING
TECH PACK AUTHOR	LAURIE VAN JONSSON			

MANUFACTURING

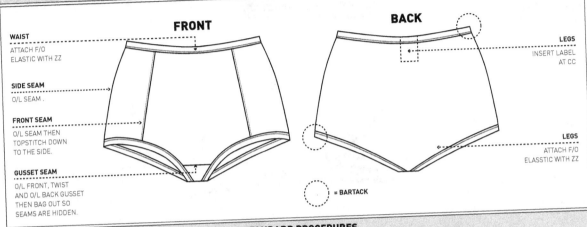

WAIST — ATTACH F/O ELASTIC WITH ZZ

SIDE SEAM — O/L SEAM.

FRONT SEAM — O/L SEAM THEN TOPSTITCH DOWN TO THE SIDE.

GUSSET SEAM — O/L FRONT, TWIST AND O/L BACK GUSSET THEN BAG OUT SO SEAMS ARE HIDDEN.

LEGS — INSERT LABEL AT CC

LEGS — ATTACH F/O ELASSTIC WITH ZZ

◌ = BARTACK

STANDARD PROCEDURES

1. GARMENTS WITH NEEDLE DAMAGED WILL NOT BE ACCEPTED. NEEDLES MUST BE CHECKED THROUGHOUT PRODUCTION.
2. PLEASE ENSURE ALL CUTTING KNIVES ON MACHINES ARE SHARPENED AND CLEANED AT ALL TIMES WHILE IN PRODUCTION.
3. MUST USE BULK STRETCH YARNS AT ALL TIMES TO PREVENT CRACKING OF STITCHES.
4. ALLOW STRETCH FABRIC TO RELAX BEFORE CUTTING.

LACE BACK BRIEF

TECH PACK

DATE	01 / 12 / 2015	CUSTOMER		HTBALD
STYLE NUMBER	0000004	FACTORY		UK
DESCRIPTION	LACE BACK BRIEF	COLOUR		BLACK: LACE, ELASTIC
PO NUMBER	TBC			BEIGE: MESH GUSSET LINING
SIZE RANGE	SIZE 8 - 12			
TECH PACK AUTHOR	LAURIE VAN JONSSON			

MANUFACTURING

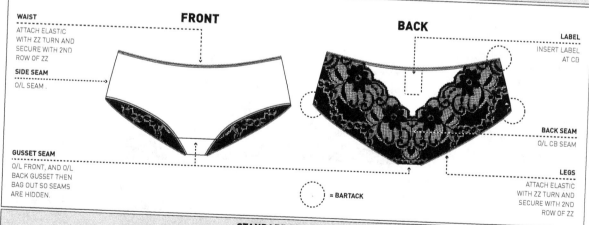

WAIST — ATTACH ELASTIC WITH ZZ TURN AND SECURE WITH 2ND ROW OF ZZ

SIDE SEAM — O/L SEAM.

GUSSET SEAM — O/L FRONT, AND O/L BACK GUSSET THEN BAG OUT SO SEAMS ARE HIDDEN.

LABEL — INSERT LABEL AT CB

BACK SEAM — O/L CB SEAM

LEGS — ATTACH ELASTIC WITH ZZ TURN AND SECURE WITH 2ND ROW OF ZZ

◌ = BARTACK

STANDARD PROCEDURES

1. GARMENTS WITH NEEDLE DAMAGED WILL NOT BE ACCEPTED. NEEDLES MUST BE CHECKED THROUGHOUT PRODUCTION.
2. PLEASE ENSURE ALL CUTTING KNIVES ON MACHINES ARE SHARPENED AND CLEANED AT ALL TIMES WHILE IN PRODUCTION.
3. MUST USE BULK STRETCH YARNS AT ALL TIMES TO PREVENT CRACKING OF STITCHES.
4. ALLOW STRETCH FABRIC TO RELAX BEFORE CUTTING.

HIGH APEX BRA FRONT

TECH PACK

DATE	01 / 12 / 2015	CUSTOMER	HTBALD
STYLE NUMBER	0000007	FACTORY	UK
DESCRIPTION	HIGH APEX BRA	COLOUR	GREY: CUPS, STRAPS, EDGE LACE
PO NUMBER	TBC		BURGUNDY: UNDERBAND, WING,
SIZE RANGE	SIZE XS, S, M, L		ELASTICS, HOOK & EYES, RINGS
TECH PACK AUTHOR	LAURIE VAN JONSSON		& SLIDES.

MANUFACTURING FRONT OF BRA

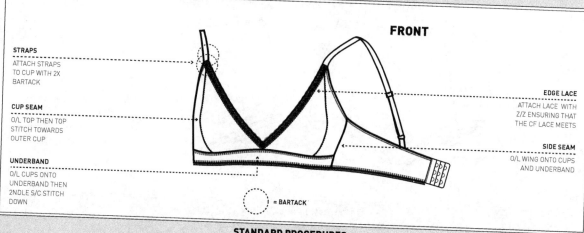

STRAPS
ATTACH STRAPS TO CUP WITH 2X BARTACK

CUP SEAM
O/L TOP THEN TOP STITCH TOWARDS OUTER CUP

UNDERBAND
O/L CUPS ONTO UNDERBAND THEN 2NDLE S/C STITCH DOWN

EDGE LACE
ATTACH LACE WITH Z/Z ENSURING THAT THE CF LACE MEETS

SIDE SEAM
O/L WING ONTO CUPS AND UNDERBAND

◯ = BARTACK

STANDARD PROCEDURES

1. GARMENTS WITH NEEDLE DAMAGED WILL NOT BE ACCEPTED. NEEDLES MUST BE CHECKED THROUGHOUT PRODUCTION.
2. PLEASE ENSURE ALL CUTTING KNIVES ON MACHINES ARE SHARPENED AND CLEANED AT ALL TIMES WHILE IN PRODUCTION.
3. MUST USE BULK STRETCH YARNS AT ALL TIMES TO PREVENT CRACKING OF STITCHES.
4. ALLOW STRETCH FABRIC TO RELAX BEFORE CUTTING.

HIGH APEX BRA BACK

TECH PACK

		CUSTOMER	HTBALD
DATE	01 / 12 / 2015	FACTORY	UK
STYLE NUMBER	0000004	COLOUR	GREY: CUPS, STRAPS, EDGE LACE
DESCRIPTION	HIGH APEX BRA		BURGUNDY: UNDERBAND, WING,
PO NUMBER	TBC		ELASTICS, HOOK & EYES, RINGS
SIZE RANGE	SIZE XS, S, M, L		& SLIDES.
TECH PACK AUTHOR	LAURIE VAN JONSSON		

MANUFACTURING BACK OF BRA

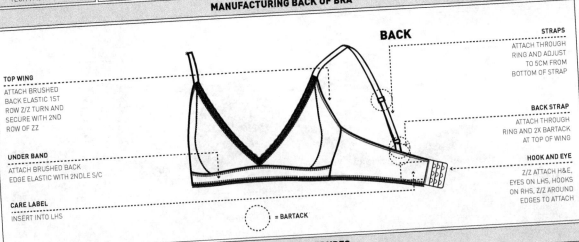

TOP WING
ATTACH BRUSHED BACK ELASTIC 1ST ROW Z/Z TURN AND SECURE WITH 2ND ROW OF ZZ

UNDER BAND
ATTACH BRUSHED BACK EDGE ELASTIC WITH 2NDLE S/C

CARE LABEL
INSERT INTO LHS

STRAPS
ATTACH THROUGH RING AND ADJUST TO 5CM FROM BOTTOM OF STRAP

BACK STRAP
ATTACH THROUGH RING AND 2X BARTACK AT TOP OF WING

HOOK AND EYE
Z/Z ATTACH H&E, EYES ON LHS, HOOKS ON RHS, Z/Z AROUND EDGES TO ATTACH

◯ = BARTACK

STANDARD PROCEDURES

1. GARMENTS WITH NEEDLE DAMAGED WILL NOT BE ACCEPTED. NEEDLES MUST BE CHECKED THROUGHOUT PRODUCTION.
2. PLEASE ENSURE ALL CUTTING KNIVES ON MACHINES ARE SHARPENED AND CLEANED AT ALL TIMES WHILE IN PRODUCTION.
3. MUST USE BULK STRETCH YARNS AT ALL TIMES TO PREVENT CRACKING OF STITCHES.
4. ALLOW STRETCH FABRIC TO RELAX BEFORE CUTTING.

UNDERWIRE BRA FRONT

TECH PACK

DATE	01 / 12 / 2015	CUSTOMER		HTBALD
STYLE NUMBER	0000008	FACTORY		UK
DESCRIPTION	UNDERWIRED BRA	COLOUR		BLACK: BINDING, RINGS, & SLIDES
PO NUMBER	TBC			HOOK & EYE, ELASTICS
SIZE RANGE	SIZE 32A-C, 34A-C, 36A-C			NAVY: WING, CUPS, UNDERBAND
TECH PACK AUTHOR	LAURIE VAN JONSSON			DENIER, STRAPS, UNDERWIRE CASING.

MANUFACTURING FRONT OF BRA

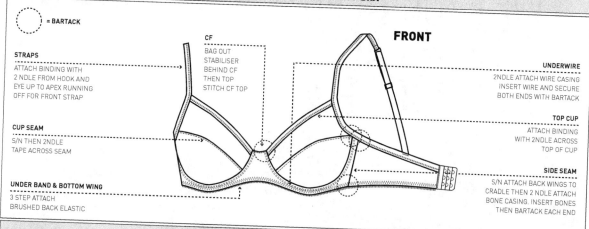

○ = BARTACK

STRAPS
ATTACH BINDING WITH 2 NDLE FROM HOOK AND EYE UP TO APEX RUNNING OFF FOR FRONT STRAP

CUP SEAM
S/N THEN 2NDLE TAPE ACROSS SEAM

UNDER BAND & BOTTOM WING
3 STEP ATTACH BRUSHED BACK ELASTIC

CF
BAG OUT STABILISER BEHIND CF THEN TOP STITCH CF TOP

FRONT

UNDERWIRE
2NDLE ATTACH WIRE CASING INSERT WIRE AND SECURE BOTH ENDS WITH BARTACK

TOP CUP
ATTACH BINDING WITH 2NDLE ACROSS TOP OF CUP

SIDE SEAM
S/N ATTACH BACK WINGS TO CRADLE THEN 2 NDLE ATTACH BONE CASING. INSERT BONES THEN BARTACK EACH END

STANDARD PROCEDURES

1. GARMENTS WITH NEEDLE DAMAGED WILL NOT BE ACCEPTED. NEEDLES MUST BE CHECKED THROUGHOUT PRODUCTION.
2. PLEASE ENSURE ALL CUTTING KNIVES ON MACHINES ARE SHARPENED AND CLEANED AT ALL TIMES WHILE IN PRODUCTION.
3. MUST USE BULK STRETCH YARNS AT ALL TIMES TO PREVENT CRACKING OF STITCHES.
4. ALLOW STRETCH FABRIC TO RELAX BEFORE CUTTING.

UNDERWIRE BRA BACK

TECH PACK

		CUSTOMER		HTBALD
DATE	01 / 12 / 2015	FACTORY		UK
STYLE NUMBER	0000008	COLOUR		BLACK: BINDING, RINGS, & SLIDES
DESCRIPTION	UNDERWIRED BRA			HOOK & EYE, ELASTICS
PO NUMBER	TBC			NAVY: WING, CUPS, UNDERBAND
SIZE RANGE	SIZE 32A-C, 34A-C, 36A-C			DENIER, STRAPS, UNDERWIRE CASING.
TECH PACK AUTHOR	LAURIE VAN JONSSON			

MANUFACTURING BACK OF BRA

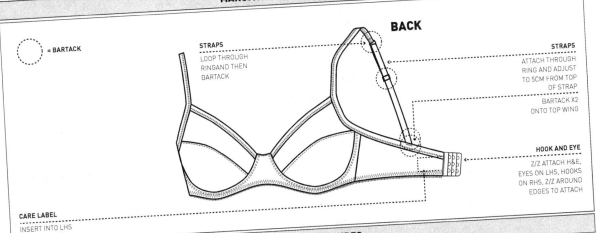

○ = BARTACK

STRAPS
LOOP THROUGH RING AND THEN BARTACK

BACK

STRAPS
ATTACH THROUGH RING AND ADJUST TO 5CM FROM TOP OF STRAP

BARTACK X2 ONTO TOP WING

HOOK AND EYE
Z/Z ATTACH H&E, EYES ON LHS, HOOKS ON RHS, Z/Z AROUND EDGES TO ATTACH

CARE LABEL
INSERT INTO LHS

STANDARD PROCEDURES

1. GARMENTS WITH NEEDLE DAMAGED WILL NOT BE ACCEPTED. NEEDLES MUST BE CHECKED THROUGHOUT PRODUCTION.
2. PLEASE ENSURE ALL CUTTING KNIVES ON MACHINES ARE SHARPENED AND CLEANED AT ALL TIMES WHILE IN PRODUCTION.
3. MUST USE BULK STRETCH YARNS AT ALL TIMES TO PREVENT CRACKING OF STITCHES.
4. ALLOW STRETCH FABRIC TO RELAX BEFORE CUTTING.

WHY YOU NEED A TECH PACK TO CHOOSE A MANUFACTURER

Finding the right manufacturer for your garments may take a lot of time and effort, but it's worth putting in the legwork. Don't just go with the first, or cheapest, manufacturing company you find. Look at a variety, and examine their production lines, weighing up how busy and how efficient they are.

There are two main routes for choosing a manufacturer; a larger, more recognised company will have extensive experience and expertise in your field. A smaller, less established manufacturing company might be able to dedicate more time and energy to your business.

The Internet is a good place to start your search, but don't rely solely on it. Visit the factory also.

The tech pack greatly comes in to use when getting a quote for the manufacuring of your garment. There are too many variables that remain undetermined without this and a precise quote almost impossible. With your Tech Pack it gives the factory an exact guide to what is involved.

"When receiving a quote back, go through what is and what isn't included.

Even though you have a packing page in your tech pack — is packing included? Also who pays for the cost of pre-production or size samples? If you are a small company all these extra costs eat into your profits.

Questions that might help are:
What happens if you need to change the garment at a late stage?
Can they do this and just charge you extra, or will you lose your manufacturing place?

Try and think of every scenario before you commit to placing an order".

EXAMPLE OF A **TECH PACK** FOR LINGERIE

Now you know what should go into a Tech Pack, on the following pages is a full example of a Tech Pack. As stated before each company will have their own style, but you have permission to replicate any information on the following pages for your own designs.

When formatting my Tech Packs I find it easiest to use Excel, you then have the ability to copy information from page to page keeping all values as accurate and confirmed as possible.

As mentioned in chapter three, the Tech Pack will contain the following pages:

Page One: A summary page
Page Two: Construction page
Page Three: Fabric and Component page
Page Four: Label page
Page Five: Packing and Shipping page

*I have not included the Spec Sheet page, for those who want a walk through of how a Specification sheet is put together, the book 'How to Spec a bra and brief' takes you through this step-by-step.

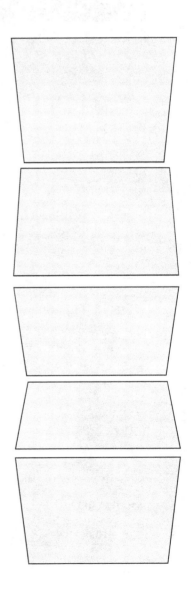

BASIC BRIEF
TECH PACK

BASIC BRIEF SUMMARY PAGE — TECH PACK

DATE	01 / 12 / 2015	CUSTOMER	HTBALD
STYLE NUMBER	0000002	FACTORY	UK
DESCRIPTION	BASIC BRIEF	COLOUR	ALL RED INCLUDING COMPONENTS
PO NUMBER	TBC		
SIZE RANGE	SIZE 8 - 12		
TECH PACK AUTHOR	LAURIE VAN JONSSON		

PRODUCTION

CHECKLIST			IMAGE
ITEM	DONE	COMMENT	
FABRIC CHOSEN	✓		
COLOUR SWATCHES		AWAITING SWATCHES FROM FACTORY	
ARTWORK			
TRIMS APPROVED			
SIZE SPEC	✓		
PACKAGING			
PATTERNS	✓		
SAMPLE APPROVED			
PP SAMPLE			
SHIPPING SAMPLES			
DELIVERY DATE	15 / 07 / 2016		

IMPORTANT INFORMATION

RELATED STYLE NUMBER IS :

BASIC BRIEF

TECH PACK

DATE	01 / 12 / 2015	CUSTOMER	HTBALD
STYLE NUMBER	0000002	FACTORY	UK
DESCRIPTION	HIGH WAISTED BRIEF	COLOUR	ALL RED INCLUDING COMPONENTS
PO NUMBER	TBC		
SIZE RANGE	SIZE 8 - 12		
TECH PACK AUTHOR	LAURIE VAN JONSSON		

MANUFACTURING

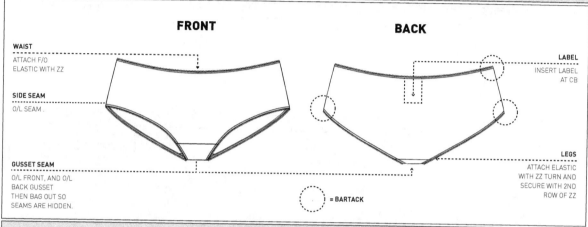

FRONT **BACK**

WAIST — ATTACH F/O ELASTIC WITH ZZ

SIDE SEAM — O/L SEAM.

GUSSET SEAM — O/L FRONT, AND O/L BACK GUSSET THEN BAG OUT SO SEAMS ARE HIDDEN.

LABEL — INSERT LABEL AT CB

LEGS — ATTACH ELASTIC WITH ZZ TURN AND SECURE WITH 2ND ROW OF ZZ

◯ = BARTACK

STANDARD PROCEDURES

1. GARMENTS WITH NEEDLE DAMAGED WILL NOT BE ACCEPTED. NEEDLES MUST BE CHECKED THROUGHOUT PRODUCTION.
2. PLEASE ENSURE ALL CUTTING KNIVES ON MACHINES ARE SHARPENED AND CLEANED AT ALL TIMES WHILE IN PRODUCTION.
3. MUST USE BULK STRETCH YARNS AT ALL TIMES TO PREVENT CRACKING OF STITCHES.
4. ALLOW STRETCH FABRIC TO RELAX BEFORE CUTTING.

BASIC BRA FABRIC SHEET

TECH PACK

DATE	01 / 12 / 2015	CUSTOMER	HTBALD
STYLE NUMBER	0000002	FACTORY	UK
DESCRIPTION	BASIC BRA	COLOUR	ALL RED INCLUING COMPONENTS
PO NUMBER	TBC		
SIZE RANGE	SIZE 8 - 12		
TECH PACK AUTHOR	LAURIE VAN JONSSON		

TRIMS

FABRIC INFORMATION
- ARTICLE NUMBER: TBC
- DESCRIPTION: MESH
- FIBRE CONTENT: 97% Nylon / 3% Elastane

POSITION: FRONT, BACK and OUTER GUSSET

FABRIC INFORMATION
- ARTICLE NUMBER: TBC
- DESCRIPTION: GUSSET LINING
- FIBRE CONTENT: 100% Cotton

POSITION: INNER GUSSET

FABRIC INFORMATION
- ARTICLE NUMBER:
- DESCRIPTION:
- FIBRE CONTENT:

POSITION:

STANDARD PROCEDURES

1. GARMENTS WITH NEEDLE DAMAGED WILL NOT BE ACCEPTED. NEEDLES MUST BE CHECKED THROUGHOUT PRODUCTION.
2. PLEASE ENSURE ALL CUTTING KNIVES ON MACHINES ARE SHARPENED AND CLEANED AT ALL TIMES WHILE IN PRODUCTION.
3. MUST USE BULK STRETCH YARNS AT ALL TIMES TO PREVENT CRACKING OF STITCHES.
4. ALLOW STRETCH FABRIC TO RELAX BEFORE CUTTING.

BASIC BRIEF TRIM

TECH PACK

DATE	01 / 12 / 2015	CUSTOMER	HTBALD
STYLE NUMBER	0000002	FACTORY	UK
DESCRIPTION	BASIC BRIEF	COLOUR	ALL RED INCLUDING COMPONENTS
PO NUMBER	TBC		
SIZE RANGE	SIZE 8 - 12		
TECH PACK AUTHOR	LAURIE VAN JONSSON		

TRIMS

LACE	ELASTIC	BOWS
ARTICLE NUMBER: TBC COMPOSITION: TBC PLACEMENT: WAIST AND LEGS SOURCING GUIDELINES -	ARTICLE NUMBER: COMPOSITION: PLACEMENT: SOURCING GUIDELINES -	ARTICLE NUMBER: COMPOSITION: PLACEMENT: SOURCING GUIDELINES -
RINGS	**SLIDES**	**HOOK AND EYES**
ARTICLE NUMBER: COMPOSITION: PLACEMENT: SOURCING GUIDELINES -	ARTICLE NUMBER: COMPOSITION: PLACEMENT: SOURCING GUIDELINES -	ARTICLE NUMBER: COMPOSITION: PLACEMENT: SOURCING GUIDELINES -

STANDARD PROCEDURES

1. GARMENTS WITH NEEDLE DAMAGED WILL NOT BE ACCEPTED. NEEDLES MUST BE CHECKED THROUGHOUT PRODUCTION.
PLEASE ENSURE ALL CUTTING KNIVES ON MACHINES ARE SHARPENED AND CLEANED AT ALL TIMES WHILE IN PRODUCTION.
PREVENT CRACKING OF STITCHES.

BASIC BRIEF LABEL Sheet

TECH PACK

DATE	01 / 12 / 2015	CUSTOMER	HTBALD
STYLE NUMBER	0000002	FACTORY	UK
DESCRIPTION	BASIC BRIEF	COLOUR	ALL RED INCLUDING COMPONENTS
PO NUMBER	TBC		
SIZE RANGE	SIZE 8 - 12		
TECH PACK AUTHOR	LAURIE VAN JONSSON		

ACCESSORIES

SEW IN LABEL		SWING TICKET	
DESCRIPTION	PRINTED SEW IN CARE LABEL	DESCRIPTION	SWING TICKET
PO NUMBER	SEW IN CB OF BRIEFS	POSITION	KIMBEL THROUGH CB LABEL

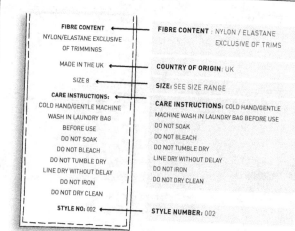

FRONT

BACK

BASIC BRIEF PACKING Sheet

TECH PACK

DATE	01 / 12 / 2015	CUSTOMER	HTBALD
STYLE NUMBER	0000002	FACTORY	UK
DESCRIPTION	BASIC BRIEF	COLOUR	ALL RED INCLUDING COMPONENTS
PO NUMBER	TBC		
SIZE RANGE	SIZE 8 - 12		
TECH PACK AUTHOR	LAURIE VAN JONSSON		

ACCESSORIES

PACKING QUANTITIES

PLEASE PACK THE GARMENTS IN THE FOLLOWING QUANTITIES

RATIO PACK BREAK DOWN

SIZE	8	10	12	TOTAL
	1	2	1	4

EXTRA INFORMATION

PLEASE ENSURE ALL PACKAGING IS ODOURLESS

DARTED SOFT BRA

TECH PACK

DARTED SOFT BRA PACKING Sheet — TECH PACK

DATE	01 / 12 / 2015	CUSTOMER	HTBALD
STYLE NUMBER	0000002	FACTORY	UK
DESCRIPTION	DARTED SOFT BRA	COLOUR	ALL RED INCLUDING COMPONENTS
PO NUMBER	TBC		
SIZE RANGE	XS, S, M, L		
TECH PACK AUTHOR	LAURIE VAN JONSSON		

PRODUCTION CHECKLIST

ITEM	DONE	COMMENT
FABRIC CHOSEN	✓	
COLOUR SWATCHES		AWAITING SWATCHES FROM FACTORY
ARTWORK		
TRIMS APPROVED		
SIZE SPEC	✓	
PACKAGING		
PATTERNS	✓	
SAMPLE APPROVED		
PP SAMPLE		
SHIPPING SAMPLES		

DELIVERY DATE: 15 / 07 / 2016

IMPORTANT INFORMATION

RELATED STYLE NUMBER IS : 002

SWATCH COLOUR

DARTED SOFT BRA FRONT — TECH PACK

DATE	01 / 12 / 2015	CUSTOMER	HTBALD
STYLE NUMBER	0000009	FACTORY	UK
DESCRIPTION	DARTED SOFT BRA	COLOUR	RED: ALL FABRICS AND COMPONENTS
PO NUMBER	TBC		
SIZE RANGE	SIZE XS, S, M, L		
TECH PACK AUTHOR	LAURIE VAN JONSSON		

MANUFACTURING FRONT OF BRA

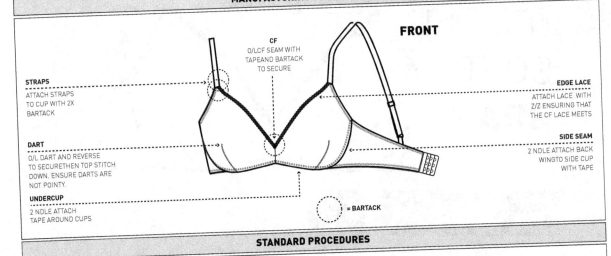

FRONT

CF — O/LCF SEAM WITH TAPE AND BARTACK TO SECURE

STRAPS — ATTACH STRAPS TO CUP WITH 2X BARTACK

DART — O/L DART AND REVERSE TO SECURE THEN TOP STITCH DOWN. ENSURE DARTS ARE NOT POINTY.

UNDERCUP — 2 NDLE ATTACH TAPE AROUND CUPS

EDGE LACE — ATTACH LACE WITH Z/Z ENSURING THAT THE CF LACE MEETS

SIDE SEAM — 2 NDLE ATTACH BACK WING TO SIDE CUP WITH TAPE

○ = BARTACK

STANDARD PROCEDURES

1. GARMENTS WITH NEEDLE DAMAGED WILL NOT BE ACCEPTED. NEEDLES MUST BE CHECKED THROUGHOUT PRODUCTION.
2. PLEASE ENSURE ALL CUTTING KNIVES ON MACHINES ARE SHARPENED AND CLEANED AT ALL TIMES WHILE IN PRODUCTION.
3. MUST USE BULK STRETCH YARNS AT ALL TIMES TO PREVENT CRACKING OF STITCHES.
4. ALLOW STRETCH FABRIC TO RELAX BEFORE CUTTING.

DARTED SOFT BRA BACK — TECH PACK

DATE	01 / 12 / 2015	CUSTOMER	HTBALD
STYLE NUMBER	0000009	FACTORY	UK
DESCRIPTION	DARTED SOFT BRA	COLOUR	RED: ALL FABRICS AND COMPONENTS
PO NUMBER	TBC		
SIZE RANGE	SIZE XS, S, M, L		
TECH PACK AUTHOR	LAURIE VAN JONSSON		

MANUFACTURING BACK OF BRA

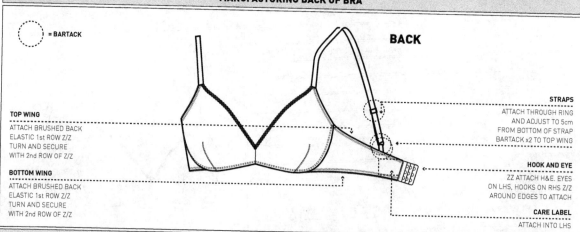

○ = BARTACK

BACK

TOP WING — ATTACH BRUSHED BACK ELASTIC 1st ROW Z/Z TURN AND SECURE WITH 2nd ROW OF Z/Z

BOTTOM WING — ATTACH BRUSHED BACK ELASTIC 1st ROW Z/Z TURN AND SECURE WITH 2nd ROW OF Z/Z

STRAPS — ATTACH THROUGH RING AND ADJUST TO 5cm FROM BOTTOM OF STRAP BARTACK x2 TO TOP WING

HOOK AND EYE — ZZ ATTACH H&E. EYES ON LHS, HOOKS ON RHS Z/Z AROUND EDGES TO ATTACH

CARE LABEL — ATTACH INTO LHS

STANDARD PROCEDURES

1. GARMENTS WITH NEEDLE DAMAGED WILL NOT BE ACCEPTED. NEEDLES MUST BE CHECKED THROUGHOUT PRODUCTION.
2. PLEASE ENSURE ALL CUTTING KNIVES ON MACHINES ARE SHARPENED AND CLEANED AT ALL TIMES WHILE IN PRODUCTION.
3. MUST USE BULK STRETCH YARNS AT ALL TIMES TO PREVENT CRACKING OF STITCHES.
4. ALLOW STRETCH FABRIC TO RELAX BEFORE CUTTING.

DARTED SOFT BRA FABRICS SHEET

TECH PACK

DATE	01 / 12 / 2015	CUSTOMER	HTBALD
STYLE NUMBER	0000009	FACTORY	UK
DESCRIPTION	BASIC BRA	COLOUR	ALL RED INCLUING COMPONENTS
PO NUMBER	TBC		
SIZE RANGE	SIZE XS, S, M, L		
TECH PACK AUTHOR	LAURIE VAN JONSSON		

TRIMS

FABRIC INFORMATION

ARTICLE NUMBER:	TBC	**POSITION**
DESCRIPTION:	MESH	CUPS AND WING
FIBRE CONTENT:	97% Nylon / 3% Elastane	

FABRIC INFORMATION

ARTICLE NUMBER:	TBC	**POSITION**
DESCRIPTION:	EDGE LACE	ALONG TOP CUP
FIBRE CONTENT:	100% Cotton	

FABRIC INFORMATION

ARTICLE NUMBER:		**POSITION**
DESCRIPTION:		
FIBRE CONTENT:		

STANDARD PROCEDURES

1. GARMENTS WITH NEEDLE DAMAGED WILL NOT BE ACCEPTED. NEEDLES MUST BE CHECKED THROUGHOUT PRODUCTION.
2. PLEASE ENSURE ALL CUTTING KNIVES ON MACHINES ARE SHARPENED AND CLEANED AT ALL TIMES.
3. MUST USE BULK STRETCH YARNS AT ALL TIMES TO PREVENT CRACKING OF STITCHES.
4. ALLOW STRETCH FABRIC TO RELAX BEFORE CUTTING.

DARTED SOFT BRA TRIMS SHEET

DATE	01 / 12 / 2015	CUSTOMER	HTBALD
STYLE NUMBER	0000009	FACTORY	UK
DESCRIPTION	SOFT DARTED BRA	COLOUR	RED: ALL FABRICS AND COMPONENTS
PO NUMBER	TBC		
SIZE RANGE	SIZE XS, S, M, L		
TECH PACK AUTHOR	LAURIE VAN JONSSON		

TRIMS

BRA STRAPPING	10 MM BRUSH BACK ELASTIC	PLASTIC BONING
ARTICLE NUMBER: TBC	ARTICLE NUMBER: TBC	ARTICLE NUMBER: N/A
COMPOSITION: TBC	COMPOSITION: TBC	PLACEMENT:
PLACEMENT: FRONT LEADING TO BACK STRAP	SIDE SEAMS: BOTTOM & TOP WING LEADING TO CUP	SIDE SEAMS:

CUPS	UNDERWIRE	11MM WIRE CASING
ARTICLE NUMBER: N/A	ARTICLE NUMBER: N?A	ARTICLE NUMBER: N/A
COMPOSITION:	COMPOSITION:	COMPOSITION:
PLACEMENT:	PLACEMENT:	PLACEMENT:

12MM RINGS	12MM SLIDES	HOOK AND EYES
ARTICLE NUMBER TBC (NYLON COATED):	ARTICLE NUMBER: TBC (NYLON COATED)	ARTICLE NUMBER:
PLACEMENT: ADJUSTABLE STRAP AT BACK	PLACEMENT: ADJUSTABLE STRAP	COMPOSITION: 100% NYLON
		PLACEMENT: AT BACK

STANDARD PROCEDURES

DARTED SOFT BRA LABEL Sheet — TECH PACK

DATE	01 / 12 / 2015
STYLE NUMBER	0000009
DESCRIPTION	DARTED SOFT BRA
PO NUMBER	TBC
SIZE RANGE	SIZE XS, S, M, L
TECH PACK AUTHOR	LAURIE VAN JONSSON

CUSTOMER	HTBALD
FACTORY	UK
COLOUR	ALL RED INCLUDING COMPONENTS

ACCESSORIES

SEW IN LABEL

DESCRIPTION	PRINTED SEW IN CARE LABEL
PO NUMBER	SEW LHS BACK OF BRAS UNDER EYES

FIBRE CONTENT: NYLON/ELASTANE EXCLUSIVE OF TRIMMINGS
MADE IN THE UK
SIZE M
CARE INSTRUCTIONS: COLD HAND/GENTLE MACHINE WASH IN LAUNDRY BAG BEFORE USE
DO NOT SOAK
DO NOT BLEACH
DO NOT TUMBLE DRY
LINE DRY WITHOUT DELAY
DO NOT IRON
DO NOT DRY CLEAN
STYLE NO: 002

FIBRE CONTENT: NYLON / ELASTANE EXCLUSIVE OF TRIMS
COUNTRY OF ORIGIN: UK
SIZE: SEE SIZE RANGE
CARE INSTRUCTIONS: COLD HAND/GENTLE MACHINE WASH IN LAUNDRY BAG BEFORE USE
DO NOT SOAK
DO NOT BLEACH
DO NOT TUMBLE DRY
LINE DRY WITHOUT DELAY
DO NOT IRON
DO NOT DRY CLEAN
STYLE NUMBER: 009

SWING TICKET

DESCRIPTION	SWING TICKET
POSITION	KIMBEL THROUGH CB LABEL

FRONT — CONSTRUCTED & HANDMADE BY Lvj — HOW TO BECOME A LINGERIE DESIGNER
SIZE: SEE SIZE RANGE
COO — MADE IN THE UK

BACK — MADE IN THE UK
SIZE _ M
£42.00
BARCODE STICKER INCLUDING PRICE

DARTED SOFT BRA PACKING Sheet — TECH PACK

DATE	01 / 12 / 2015
STYLE NUMBER	0000009
DESCRIPTION	DARTED SOFT BRA
PO NUMBER	TBC
SIZE RANGE	SIZE XS - L
TECH PACK AUTHOR	LAURIE VAN JONSSON

CUSTOMER	HTBALD
FACTORY	UK
COLOUR	ALL RED INCLUDING COMPONENTS

ACCESSORIES

PACKING QUANTITIES

PLEASE PACK THE GARMENTS IN THE FOLLOWING QUANTITIES

RATIO PACK BREAK DOWN

SIZE				TOTAL
XS	S	M	L	
1	2	2	1	6

EXTRA INFORMATION

PLEASE ENSURE ALL PACKAGING IS ODOURLESS

CONCLUSION

Don't be disheartened if when you write your Tech Pack that it take ages to complete. Once you complete style upon style it will get a lot quicker especially if you make yourself a simple template to insert the information.

Getting the tech pack correct at the start will save you time further down the road, and if you don't have all the information, insert it when you receive it, otherwise you will find yourself wading through pages and pages of information to find the correct source. If any changes are made, highlight and date what you have changed. There's nothing more frustrating wondering whether you have done the next time you look at it.

Above all that, be excited that you've just completed one of the final steps to get your garment manufactured. That idea you started out with now can be picked up by any factory and completed to exactly how you want it. You designing lingerie is no longer a pipe dream.

If you find yourself completely stuck or wish for some assistance or have any questions, a contact page can be found at www.howtobecomealingeriedesigner.com. I will answer the best I can and if I don't have the right answers I will direct you where you can find them. There is also a blog that you can follow, which is updated with tips, advice and articles about Lingerie.

CHAPTER 2

HOW TO SPEC A BRA & BRIEF

The problem?

You've got one size ready (the sealer)!

How much should you increase or decrease your one size to write your spec..?

"From my first ever job designing lingerie and swimwear for UK High Streets (2000) to freelancing internationally (2015), the basic rules for grading standard sizes haven't changed. What you start to learn about specification sheets, you build on that knowledge through-out the years.

That's not to say that all lingerie is graded exactly the same. Different companies may provide you with different measurements in which they want their garments graded to.

For example some companies increase the side seam per size on a brief, others adjust the side measurement according to the fabric and other companies keep the side seam the same across all sizes.

All that knowledge comes from experience. The best way to learn how to write a specification sheet is start with the basics and as you learn more about lingerie, you'll know from the design if you have to increase the side seam per size or keep it consistent.

Once you learn the grade rules for your spec you can build upon them, and transform your design from paper into the most beautiful, incredible lingerie in a multitude of sizes."

HOW TO SPEC A
BRA AND BRIEF

Specification sheets or 'spec sheets' as they are known provide all the information that takes a pattern and turns it into a finished garment. Some companies may call 'tech packs' 'spec sheets'.

In this book, so there is no confusion, we will be referencing spec sheets as the sizing information needed by the factory to ensure every garment comes up to spec (measures the correct size). The spec sheets in this book are designed to include technical diagrams and garment measurements. The main goal of any spec sheet is to provide the details of how the garment is sized.

Each company has their own format, but the information runs along the same lines and is just tailored to the company needs. Learning how to measure clothing will be one of most important skills you can have, and will save errors in the future.

This book will......

Explain why writing a spec sheet is important and who uses them.

Show you how to write a graded specification sheet.

Will share industry standard grade rules.

Provide you with step-by step instructions and diagrams.

Give you permission to replicate any of the spec examples used in the book.

AN INTRODUCTION TO SPEC SHEETS

So how do you write a specification sheet after you've designed your lingerie?

A specification can be produced two ways:

1 The designer produces a specification sheet for the pattern maker to work from, and then a pattern is drafted from the measurements.

2 A first pattern is drafted from a sketch, a sample made, and measurements taken off the garment to make the spec.

This book shall look at the first option. Though whichever way you write the specification sheet, the final measurements will be measured from the 'sealer', which is also called a pre-production sample (or PP sample).

Meaning that measurements may change from the initial spec. To reach the seal sample stage, a first fit sample is made; alterations are put into effect (if needed) and then re-fitted. This is classed as production development.

A seal sample is a sample of the final garment. This sample should represent what the final piece will look like. In some companies a seal sample may have a tag on it, to identify it, (usually a red or gold tag). This sealer is sent away with the spec sheet to the factory.

When you are ready to make your own lingerie you can

1 Employ a technician to grade your pattern, write your specification sheets and complete the grade.

2 Spec (and grade the patterns yourself), ready to complete your first range.

Tip
You may need to fit the bra several times if you are just starting out

USING A SPEC SHEET

Why is learning how to write a spec sheet important?

Well spec sheets are used, as a communication between the design team, technical team and factory. The spec sheet is used in production and patternmaking to ensure the correct fit. They help prevent costly errors, and ensure that the technical team understands exactly what the designer has in mind.

A **patternmaker** when making a first pattern from a sketch; might estimate then measurements, then have a sample made, and take the measurements from this garment to produce a spec sheet. Or they might be given the spec sheet first, and draft a first pattern from this according to the measurements.

Production personnel will use the specs for developing the cost of the garment. If the cost is too high, the designer can go back to the spec and see if the garment can be scaled back, and measurements reduced.

Manufacturers use the spec sheets to estimate marker yardage (the amount of fabric used) to gain an accurate cost, and to ensure when in production that all the garments measure the same.

Quality Controllers use the spec sheets to ensure that the factory has manufactured the garments to the designer's original measurements. They will ensure that all garments are in tolerance (a measuring discrepancy given to all make-up of garments) before they are sent out to the shops.

WHAT TO WRITE ON A SPEC SHEET..!

At the top of the spec sheet it will include pertinent information such as company name, season, description, style code and production number.

It will have key measurements, dimensions of the garment in different standard sizes and a drawing of the garment.

The spec sheet will show the measurements at many key points of the garment, such as underband length on bras, front rise on briefs etc. All measurements are done front and back (apart from the bra which can be laid flat if it has hook and eyes). When designing a spec sheet, it's easier to place all POM in the same order each time.

POM stands for 'Point of measurement'

A picture is worth more than words; so for every POM reference written down on the spec sheet, use arrows on the diagram stating exactly where you are measuring. This will solve any measurement discrepancies quickly, especially if the factory you are using is abroad.

The important information such as bow placement, thread colour, type of fabric, cuttings of fabrics and trims etc would be placed in the tech pack.

MEASURING A BRIEF FOR A SPEC SHEET

There are key measurements that are taken for a Spec. Some companies have codes that are used for the same POM, by learning these codes you instantly know the POM they are referring to.
For example:
500: Waist Relaxed
501: Waist Extended etc.

Though many companies just reference each measure point by 1-10 etc or by the Alphabet.

To keep it simple the book will reference each POM by the Alphabet. Get into the habit of writing the measurements in the same order where possible. This will save you time, and help those around you if you are passing the spec on.

"There are two ways to measure your garment, either with a dressmaker's flexible tape measure, or by having ruler measurements taped to the edge of the desk. It's a personal choice; I use a combination. Anything that needs to be extended, i.e. the waist and legs of a brief or the under-band of a bra, I use the tape measure that is taped to the desk. These are the measurements where you need both hands, especially when extending the garment. Every other measurement, I use a flexible tape measure".

Check your flexible tape measure against a metal rule as over time they can stretch.

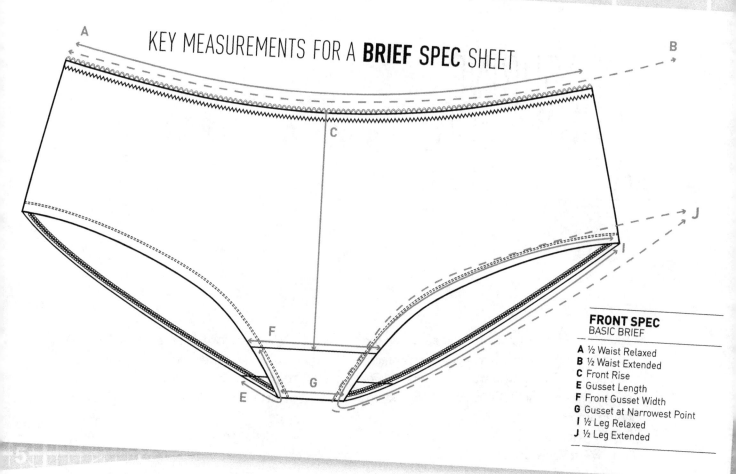

FRONT SPEC
BASIC BRIEF

- **A** ½ Waist Relaxed
- **B** ½ Waist Extended
- **C** Front Rise
- **E** Gusset Length
- **F** Front Gusset Width
- **G** Gusset at Narrowest Point
- **I** ½ Leg Relaxed
- **J** ½ Leg Extended

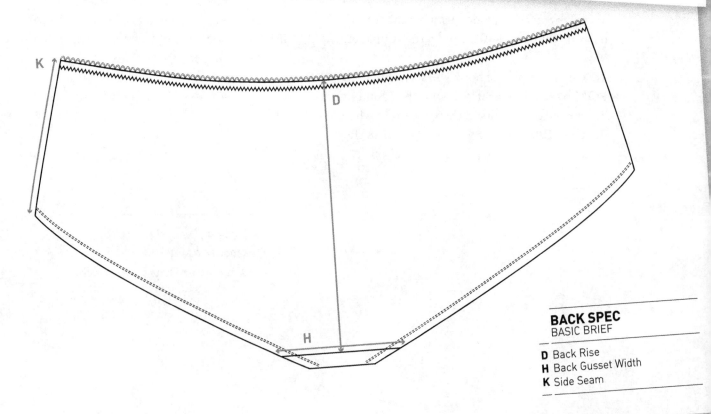

BACK SPEC
BASIC BRIEF

- **D** Back Rise
- **H** Back Gusset Width
- **K** Side Seam

A ½ Waist Relaxed
Measure from side seam to side seam along the waistband at the top edge. It's stated as ½ waist so you are not measuring around the whole waist (front and back). It's important to make this clear especially if you are passing this spec onto a pattern maker.

B ½ Waist Extended
For extended measurements, measure as above with elastic of waist fully extended.

C Front Rise
Measure down the middle of the centre front (CF) from the waist to the gusset seam (if there is no seam, measure to the natural fold of the brief). If thick elastic is used, state on spec sheet 'including elastic or excluding elastic'.

E Gusset Length (length of gusset)
On the inside of the garment, measure down the middle of the centre of the gusset, from top to bottom

F Front Gusset Width
Measure across the top of the gusset (if a triangle gusset is used then there will be no measurement). If thick elastic is used, state on the spec sheet 'including elastic or excluding elastic'.

G Gusset at Narrowest Point
Measure across the narrowest part of the gusset. This will differ from garment to garment. If thick elastic is used, state on the spec sheet 'including elastic or excluding elastic'.

I ½ Leg Relaxed
Placing the front and back legs together, measure flat along the leg opening, usually from a gusset point to the side seam. It's stated as ½ leg so you are not measuring around the whole leg opening (front and back).

J ½ Leg Extended
For extended measurements, measure as above with elastic of the leg fully extended.

When writing a spec, if you write ½ waist measurements and ½ leg measurements, it's far easier for two reasons:

1. *As both sides are the same, you only grade one side and mirror the other. With the full measurement you would have to work out the half measurement.*

2. *It's quicker for the sample machinist to check measurements. They can simply measure off the rule they have stuck on their desk in front of their machine, rather than walk a drapers tape around the waist or leg opening.*

D Back Rise
Measure down the middle of the centre back (CB) from the waist to the gusset seam (if there is no seam measure to the natural fold of the brief). If thick elastic is used, state on spec sheet 'including elastic or excluding elastic'.

H Back Gusset Width
Measure across the bottom of the gusset, usually along the back seam of the gusset, (if a triangle gusset is used then there will be no measurement). If thick elastic is used, state on the spec sheet 'including elastic or excluding elastic'.

K Side Seam Length
Measure along the side seam – where the front and back piece joins, if there is no seam measure to the natural fold of the brief. If thic elastic is used, state on the spec sheet 'including elastic or excluding elastic'.

GRADING
BRIEFS

The measurements that follow show the increase and decrease values when grading your briefs size smaller or larger from the base size.

A	½ Waist Relaxed	2.5 cm
B	½ Waist Extended	2.5 cm
C	Front Rise	1 cm
D	Back Rise	1 cm
E	Gusset Length	0 cm
F	Front Gusset Width	0 cm (can differ by 0-0.5cm)
G	Gusset at Narrowest Point	0 cm (can differ by 0-0.5cm)
H	Back Gusset Width	0 cm (can differ by 0-0.5cm)
I	½ Leg Relaxed	1.4 cm
J	½ Leg Extended	1.4 cm
K	Side Seam Length	0 cm (can differ by 0-0.5cm)

The measurements to put on your spec sheet..

This is what the measurements would look like on a Specification sheet...

SIZE SPECIFICATION			STYLE NO: 001		SUPPLIER: HOW TO BECOME A LINGERIE DESIGNER			
GARMENT DESCRIPTION :			Basic Brief					
SKETCH:	REF	POINT OF MEASUREMENT	XS	S	M	L		TOL (-)
	A	1/2 waist relaxed	-5.0	-2.5	0.0	2.5		0.5
	B	1/2 waist stretched	-5.0	-2.5	0.0	2.5		1.0
	C	Front rise	-2.0	-1.0	0.0	1.0		0.5
	D	Back rise	-2.0	-1.0	0.0	1.0		0.5
	E	Gusset length	0.0	0.0	0.0	0.0		0.5
	F	Front gusset width	-0.5	0.0	0.0	0.0		0.5
	G	Gusset at narrowest point	-0.5	0.0	0.0	0.0		0.5
	H	Back gusset width	-0.5	0.0	0.0	0.0		0.5
	I	1/2 leg relaxed	-2.8	-1.4	0.0	1.4		0.5
	J	1/2 leg stretched	-2.8	-1.4	0.0	1.4		1.0
	K	Side seam length	-0.5	0.0	0.0	0.0		0.5
	Special Instructions:							
	NAME: LVJ				DATE: 01/12/2014			

...and here is an example of actual measurements of a brief I have made.

SIZE SPECIFICATION			STYLE NO: 001		SUPPLIER: HOW TO BECOME A LINGERIE DESIGNER			
GARMENT DESCRIPTION :			Basic Brief					
SKETCH:	REF	POINT OF MEASUREMENT	XS	S	M	L		TOL (-)
	A	1/2 waist relaxed	23.4	25.9	28.4	30.9		0.5
	B	1/2 waist stretched	38.0	40.5	43.0	45.5		1
	C	Front rise	9.0	10.0	11.0	12.0		0.5
	D	Back rise	15.5	16.5	17.5	18.5		0.5
	E	Gusset length	10.7	10.7	10.7	10.7		0.5
	F	Front gusset width	5.5	6.0	6.0	6.0		0.5
	G	Gusset at narrowest point	4.5	5.0	5.0	5.0		0.5
	H	Back gusset width	6.7	7.2	7.2	7.2		0.5
	I	1/2 leg relaxed	20.7	22.1	23.5	24.9		0.5
	J	1/2 leg stretched	32.2	33.6	35.0	36.4		1
	K	Side seam length	9.8	10.3	10.3	10.3		0.5
	Special Instructions:							
	NAME: LVJ				DATE: 01/12/2014			

At the back of the book are empty versions with and without the written measurements for you to use.

THE HIGH BRIEF

The high brief follows the same grading, shown are measurements from a previous high brief I have made.

SIZE SPECIFICATION			STYLE NO: 002		SUPPLIER: HOW TO BECOME A LINGERIE DESIGNER			
GARMENT DESCRIPTION:			**Panel High Brief**					
REF	POINT OF MEASUREMENT		XS	S	M	L		TOL (-)
A	1/2 waist relaxed		23.5	26.0	28.5	31.0		0.5
B	1/2 waist stretched		39.0	41.5	44.0	46.5		1
C	Front rise (excl. elastic)		18.2	19.2	20.2	21.2		0.5
D	Back rise (excl. elastic)		24.8	25.8	26.8	27.8		0.5
E	Gusset length		14.5	14.5	14.5	14.5		0.5
F	Front gusset width (e.e)		6.8	7.3	7.3	7.3		0.5
G	Gusset at narrowest point (e.e)		5.0	5.5	5.5	5.5		0.5
H	Back gusset width (e.e)		11.5	12.0	12.0	12.0		0.5
I	1/2 leg relaxed		22.2	23.6	25.0	26.4		0.5
J	1/2 leg stretched		35.2	36.6	38.0	39.4		1
K	Side seam length (e.e)		13.5	14.0	14.0	14.0		0.5
L	Front side seam		11.2	12.2	13.2	14.2		0.5

Special Instructions:

NAME: LVJ   DATE: 01/12/2014

THE LACE BACK **BRIEF**

The same grading applies to the lace back brief, however on this brief the grade for the centre back is split into two to create an even grade. So 0.5cm is applied to the top part of the brief and 0.5cm is applied to the bottom part of the brief, (D1 & D2).

SIZE SPECIFICATION			STYLE NO: 003		SUPPLIER: HOW TO BECOME A LINGERIE DESIGNER			
GARMENT DESCRIPTION:			Galloon lace back brief					
SKETCH:	REF	POINT OF MEASUREMENT	XS	S	M	L		TOL (-)
	A	1/2 waist relaxed	23.7	26.2	28.7	31.2		0.5
	B	1/2 waist stretched	40.0	42.5	45.0	47.5		1
	C	Front rise	11.6	12.6	13.6	14.6		0.5
	D1	Mesh Back Rise	7.6	8.1	8.6	9.1		0.5
	D2	Lace Back rise	9.0	9.5	10.0	10.5		0.5
	E	Gusset length	14.0	14.0	14.0	14.0		0.5
	F	Front gusset width	6.5	7.0	7.0	7.0		0.5
	G	Gusset at narrowest point	4.3	4.8	4.8	4.8		0.5
	H	Back gusset width	11.0	11.5	11.5	11.5		0.5
	I	1/2 leg relaxed	21.8	23.2	24.6	26.0		0.5
	J	1/2 leg stretched	35.2	36.6	38.0	39.4		1
	K	Side seam length	6.0	6.5	6.5	6.5		0.5
Special Instructions:								
	NAME: LVJ			DATE: 01/12/2014				

THE G STRING

With the G-string there are slightly different measurements for the waist. The front panel and side string both grade, and the back section only grades down in the extra-small size.

The front panel grades by 1.5cm (across the top), and the side string by 3.5cm (1cm from the front and 2.5cm from the back). Although the extra-small size goes down by 3cm as the back section has already gone down by 0.5cm.

SIZE SPECIFICATION				STYLE NO: 005		SUPPLIER: HOW TO BECOME A LINGERIE DESIGNER	
GARMENT DESCRIPTION :			G-String				
SKETCH:	REF	POINT OF MEASUREMENT	XS	S	M	L	TOL (-)
	A	1/2 waist relaxed	16.0	17.5	19.0	20.5	0.5
	B	1/2 waist stretched	37.0	39.5	42.0	44.5	1
	C	Front rise	8.7	9.7	10.7	11.7	0.5
	D	Back string	13.2	14.2	15.2	16.2	0.5
	E	Gusset length	9.4	9.4	9.4	9.4	0.5
	F	Front gusset width	5.9	6.4	6.4	6.4	0.5
	G	Gusset at narrowest point	3.7	4.2	4.2	4.2	0.5
	H	Back gusset width	1.5	1.5	1.5	1.5	0.5
	I	1/2 leg relaxed	17.4	18.8	20.2	21.6	0.5
	J	1/2 leg stretched	31.2	32.6	34.0	35.4	1
	K	Back width triangle	5.0	5.5	5.5	5.5	0.5
	L	Side String	13.0	16.0	19.5	23.0	0.5

Special Instructions:

NAME: LVJ   DATE: 01/12/2014

MEASURING A BRA FOR A SHEET

" The standards I have worked with in the past for measuring bras have differed slightly from company to company. Especially when working with under-wires. Depending on the type of bra will depend on the type of wire used, which alters the grade of the wire. For example a full cup bra will have a longer wire and a different grade than a plunge wire, (which will have a shorter wire)."

Regarding the grades on the wire, this information will come from your wire supplier; you will be supplied with a wire chart, which will have templates of the wire sizes and the full grade. Those working with molded cups will have the grade information supplied for the whole cup, so you can work out the pattern and grades for the outer fabric cup.

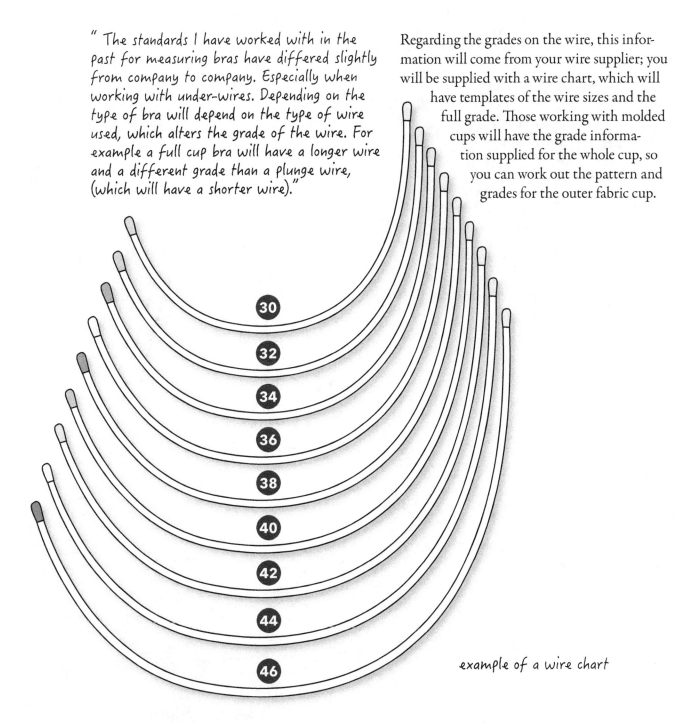

example of a wire chart

KEY BRA MEASUREMENTS

The key measurements needed to be shown on a Spec sheet for a bra

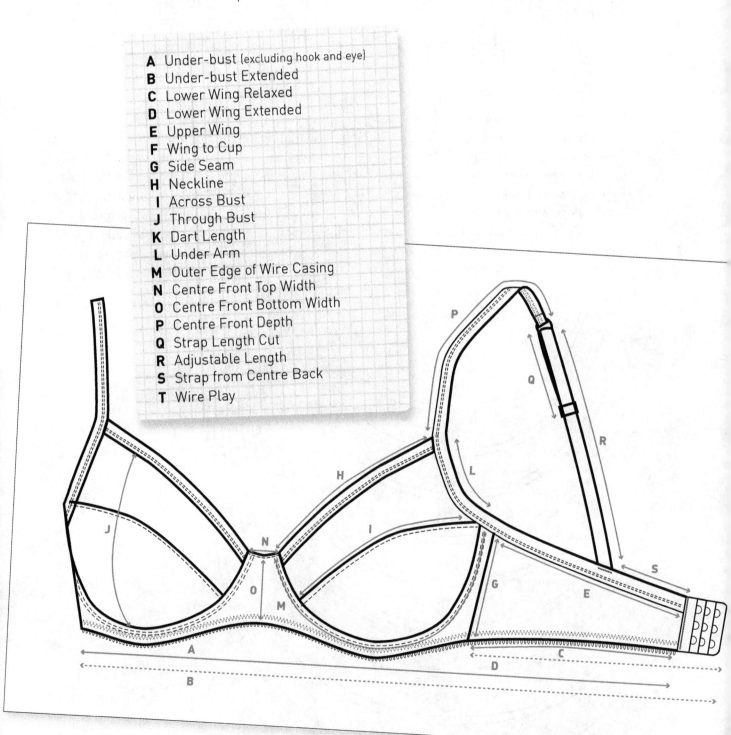

A Under-bust (excluding hook and eye)
B Under-bust Extended
C Lower Wing Relaxed
D Lower Wing Extended
E Upper Wing
F Wing to Cup
G Side Seam
H Neckline
I Across Bust
J Through Bust
K Dart Length
L Under Arm
M Outer Edge of Wire Casing
N Centre Front Top Width
O Centre Front Bottom Width
P Centre Front Depth
Q Strap Length Cut
R Adjustable Length
S Strap from Centre Back
T Wire Play

A Under-bust (excluding hook and eye)
Laying the bra flat measure along the under-band from the hook to the eye. Don't include the hook and eye in your measurements. It doesn't matter if the bra has a cradle or not (a cradle is where the centre front and wing meets under the cup).

B Under-bust Extended
Measure as above, with elastic of the under-band fully extended.

C Lower Wing Relaxed
Measure along the elastic at the bottom of the wing. Depending if the bra has a cradle or not, depends where you measure from. If the bra has no cradle, measure from the hook or eye to where the wing meets the cup. If your bra has a cradle, measure from the hook and eye to the seam join to where the wing joins the centre front or sidepiece. This may be under the cup or at the side of the cup.

D Lower Wing Extended
measure as above with elastic of the lower wing fully extended.

E Upper Wing
Measure along the top of the wing, from the hook and eye to where the wing meets the cup.

F Wing to Cup
Measure along the depth of the wing, where the wing meets the cup.

G Side Seam
Measure along the depth of the seam where the wing meets the side cradle (not on every bra will there be this measurement, it depends if you have a full wing or a wing that is split).

H Neckline
Measure the neck edge of the bra, from the apex (where the strap usually sits) to the bottom of the neck edge, if measuring an under-wire bra state whether the wire is included or excluded.

I Across Bust
Measure from the centre front across the cup through the highest point to mid-point of the wing. If there is an over-bust (horizontal) seam then measure along this.

J Through Bust
Measure from the bottom of the cup to the top of the cup through the highest point (this usually at the mid point of the neck line not the strap point). If there is a vertical seam then measure along this.

K Dart Length
Measure along the dart length of the cup, this measurement will only apply if there is a dart in the cup.

L Under Arm
Measure from the apex (where the strap meets the cup) along the underarm to the wing.

M Outer Edge of Wire Casing
Measure the outer edge of the wire casing, it's important to state where the measurement occurs and not just write 'Wire Casing'. There will be a different measurement from the inside of the wire casing. This measurement will only apply if the bra is under-wired.

N Centre Front Top Width
Measure the top of the centre front (CF) between the cups, if measuring an under-wire bra, state whether the under-wires are included or excluded in the measurements.

O Centre Front Bottom Width
Measure the bottom of the centre front (CF) between the cups.

P Centre Front Depth
Measure from the top to the bottom of the centre front (CF)

Q Strap Length Cut
This is the total length at which the strap length is cut at.

R Adjustable Length
Measure along the strap, which is doubled up as it is adjusted.

S Strap from Centre Back
Measure the distance along the top of the wing from the hook and eye to the strap. This measurement is only needed if a camisole style of strap is used (where the strap is inserted into the top of the wing).

T Wire Play
Although this isn't an actual measurement in which you are going to grade from, this measurement is important for the finished garment. It is an amount in which the wire is from the end of the wire casing. It's important to leave a gap so the wire isn't pressed against the end; otherwise the pressure would enable the wire to poke out and come through the wire casing.

STANDARD GRADING FOR BRAS

"Grading across band and cup sizes can differ depending on the style (the information in brackets are the most common grades I've worked with) so not to make things too complicated. Under-wire bras will grade as follows"

The basic soft bra grading rules can be used as a starting point, or as your actual grade. They are for sizes 8-14 or x/small – x/large. (We are keeping the extended measurement the same as the relaxed measurement and not the stretch of the elastic ratio).

A	Under-bust Relaxed:	5.0 cm
B	Under-bust Extended:	5.0 cm
C	Lower Wing Relaxed:	1.5 cm
D	Lower Wing Extended:	1.5 cm
E	Upper Wing:	1.5 cm
F	Wing to Cup:	0.5 cm
G	Side Seam:	0.5 cm
H	Neckline:	1.0 cm
I	Across Bust:	1.0 cm
J	Through Bust:	1.0 cm
K	Dart Length:	0.5 cm
L	Under Arm:	0.5 cm
M	Outer Edge of Wire Casing:	
N	Centre Front Top Width:	0 cm
O	Centre Front Bottom Width:	0 cm
P	Centre Front Depth:	0 cm
Q	Strap Length Cut:	0 cm
R	Adjustable Length:	0 cm
S	Strap from Centre Back:	0.5 cm
T	Wire Play:	-

When grading an under-wire bra, the grade will differ depending on the grade of the wire. The grade of the wire can differ usually from 1.4cm to 2.3cm, which will in turn alter the 'across and through bust' measurement.

A. Under-bust Relaxed: 5.0cm
B. Under-bust Extended: 5.0cm
C. Lower Wing Relaxed: 1.5cm [can differ between 1.0-2.0cm grade]
D. Lower Wing Extended: 1.5cm [can differ between 1.0-2.0cm grade]
E. Upper Wing: 1.5cm [can differ between 1.0-2.0cm grade]
F. Wing to Cup: 0.5cm [can differ between 0.5 -1.0cm grade]
G. Side Seam: 0.5cm
H. Neckline: 1.0cm [can differ between 0.8cm-1.3cm grade]
I. Across Bust: 1.0cm [can differ between 0.8cm-1.3cm grade]
J. Through Bust: 1.0cm [can differ between 0.8cm-1.3cm grade]
K. Dart Length: 0.5cm
L. Under Arm: 0.5cm [can differ between 0.3cm-0.6cm grade]
M. Outer Edge of Wire Casing: [can differ between 1.4cm-2.2cm grade]
N. Centre Front Top Width: 0cm [on larger cups this may in/decrease]
O. Centre Front Bottom Width: 0.cm [as above]
P. Centre Front Depth: 0cm [on larger cup sizes this may in/decrease]
Q. Strap Length Cut: 0cm
R. Adjustable Length: 0cm
S. Strap from Centre Back: 0.5cm
T. Wire Play: 1cm

The spec sheet for the darted non-wired bra is showing the Small, Medium, Large grades. Where there is no measurement that correlates to the garment it's just left blank. I am showing in the spec the total it grades by and also the measurements of an actual darted bra I have made previously.

SIZE SPECIFICATION				STYLE NO:		SUPPLIER: HOW TO BECOME A LINGERIE DESIGNER		
GARMENT DESCRIPTION :			Darted soft bra					
SKETCH:	REF	POINT OF MEASUREMENT		XS	S	M	L	TOL (-)
	A	Under-bust		-10.0	-5.0	0.0	5.0	1.0
	B	Under-bust extended		-10.0	-5.0	0.0	5.0	1.0
	C	Lower wing relaxed		-3.0	-1.5	0.0	1.5	0.5
	D	Lower wing extended		-3.0	-1.5	0.0	1.5	1.0
	E	Upper wing		-3.0	-1.5	0.0	1.5	0.5
	F	Wing to cup		-1.0	-0.5	0.0	0.5	0.5
	G	Side seam		-1.0	-0.5	0.0	0.5	0.5
	H	Neckline		-2.0	-1.0	0.0	1.0	0.5
	I	Across bust		-2.0	-1.0	0.0	1.0	0.5
	J	Through bust		-2.0	-1.0	0.0	1.0	0.5
	K	Dart length		-1.0	-0.5	0.0	0.5	0.5
	L	Under arm		-1.0	-0.5	0.0	0.5	0.5
	M	Outer edge of wire casing		0.0	0.0	0.0	0.0	0.5
	N	Centre front top width		0.0	0.0	0.0	0.0	0.3
	O	Centre front bottom width		0.0	0.0	0.0	0.0	0.3
	P	Centre front depth		0.0	0.0	0.0	0.0	0.5
	Q	Strap length cut		0.0	0.0	0.0	0.0	1.0
	R	Adjustable length		0.0	0.0	0.0	0.0	0.5
	S	Strap from back		-1.0	-0.5	0.0	0.5	0.5
		Wire play						
Special Instructions:								
	NAME:	LVJ				DATE: 01/12/2014		

SIZE SPECIFICATION				STYLE NO: 007		SUPPLIER: HOW TO BECOME A LINGERIE DESIGNER		
GARMENT DESCRIPTION :			Darted soft bra					
SKETCH:	REF	POINT OF MEASUREMENT		XS	S	M	L	TOL (-)
	A	Under-bust		48.0	53.0	58.0	63.0	1.0
	B	Under-bust extended		72.0	77.0	82.0	87.0	1.0
	C	Lower wing relaxed		14.5	16.0	17.5	19.0	0.5
	D	Lower wing extended		21.0	22.5	24.0	25.5	1.0
	E	Upper wing		13.5	15.0	16.5	18.0	0.5
	F	Wing to cup		7.5	8.0	8.5	9.0	0.5
	G							
	H	Neckline		13.7	14.7	15.7	16.7	0.5
	I	Across bust		16.2	17.2	18.2	19.2	0.5
	J	Through bust		12.7	13.7	14.7	15.7	0.5
	K	Dart length		6.0	6.5	7.0	7.5	0.5
	L	Under arm		9.0	9.5	10.0	10.5	0.5
	M							
	N							
	O							
	P	Centre front depth		3.0	3.0	3.0	3.0	0.3
	Q	Strap length cut		44.0	44.0	44.0	44.0	0.5
	R	Adjustable length		5.0	5.0	5.0	5.0	0.5
	S	Strap from back		4.5	5.0	5.5	6.0	0.5
Special Instructions:								
	NAME:	LVJ				DATE: 01/12/2014		

Spec details of a soft apex bra previously made with actual measurements in place.

SIZE SPECIFICATION		STYLE NO: 008	SUPPLIER: HOW TO BECOME A LINGERIE DESIGNER									
GARMENT DESCRIPTION : Underwire seam bra												
SKETCH:												

REF	POINT OF MEASUREMENT	32A	32B	32C	34A	34B	34C	36A	36B	36C		TOL (-)
A	Under-bust	55.0	55.0	55.0	60.0	60.0	60.0	65.0	65.0	65.0		
B	Under-bust extended	75.0	75.0	75.0	80.0	80.0	80.0	85.0	85.0	85.0		
C	Lower wing relaxed	23.6	22.1	20.6	25.1	23.6	22.1	26.6	25.1	23.6		
D	Lower wing extended	33.0	31.5	30.0	34.5	33.0	31.5	36.0	34.5	33.0		
E	Upper wing	15.3	13.8	12.3	16.8	15.3	13.8	18.3	16.8	15.3		
G	Side seam	6.0	6.5	7.0	6.5	7.0	7.5	7.0	7.5	8.0		
H	Neckline (excl. wire)	15.2	16.2	17.2	16.2	17.2	18.2	17.2	18.2	19.2		
I	Across bust	13.9	15.1	16.3	15.1	16.3	17.5	16.3	17.5	18.7		
J	Through bust	10.1	11.1	12.1	11.1	12.1	13.1	12.1	13.1	14.1		
L	Under arm	8.5	9.0	9.5	9.0	9.5	10.0	9.5	10.0	10.5		
M	Outer edge of wire casing	17.4	18.6	19.8	18.6	19.8	21.0	19.8	21.0	22.2		
N	Centre front top width (incl.wires)	2.5	2.5	2.5	2.5	2.5	2.5	2.5	2.5	2.5		
O	Centre front depth	3.7	3.7	3.7	3.7	3.7	3.7	3.7	3.7	3.7		
P	Front strap length finished at	17.0	17.0	17.0	17.0	17.0	17.0	17.0	17.0	17.0		
Q	Strap length cut	23.0	23.0	23.0	23.0	23.0	23.0	23.0	23.0	23.0		
R	Adjustable length	11.0	11.0	11.0	11.0	11.0	11.0	11.0	11.0	11.0		
S	Strap from back	4.5	5.0	5.5	4.0	4.5	5.0	3.5	4.0	4.5		
	Wire play: 1cm											

Special Instructions:

NAME: LVJ   DATE: 01/12/2014

> "For those who have read my other books 'How to become a Lingerie Designer' & 'The Anatomy of the Bra' you will recognize the cross grading table that is about to be shown. In both books cross grading is mentioned as it's such an important part of understanding how the industry grades from one size to another".

When it comes to writing a spec sheet for an underwired bra, things get a bit more complicated. Shown will be a spec sheet with cross grading measurements on. It will just show sizes A to C; as when you get into D cups, other measurements need to be independently altered, like the under arm measurement (the apex needs to be moved towards the centre of the body so the breasts don't splay out).

Cross grading a bra is when a 34B has the same cup size as a 32C however the 32C has a smaller back. A 36B bra has greater volume than a 34B as the band has increased and also the cup. See the table below to see how the sizes correlate to one and another.

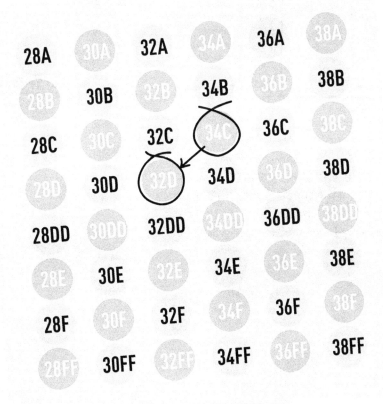

Bra sizes of 34A 34B 34C have the same size under-band, but obviously the 34A has smaller cups than the 34C. This tells you that the 34A wing will be bigger than the 34C wing, to maintain the same under-band measurement across all sizes.

SIZE SPECIFICATION		STYLE NO: 008	SUPPLIER: HOW TO BECOME A LINGERIE DESIGNER							
GARMENT DESCRIPTION :		Underwire seam bra								
SKETCH:	REF POINT OF MEASUREMENT	32A	32B	32C	34A	34B	34C	36A	36B	36C	TOL (-)

REF	POINT OF MEASUREMENT	32A	32B	32C	34A	34B	34C	36A	36B	36C
A	Under-bust	55.0	55.0	55.0	60.0	60.0	60.0	65.0	65.0	65.0
B	Under-bust extended	75.0	75.0	75.0	80.0	80.0	80.0	85.0	85.0	85.0
C	Lower wing relaxed	23.6	22.1	20.6	25.1	23.6	22.1	26.6	25.1	23.6
D	Lower wing extended	33.0	31.5	30.0	34.5	33.0	31.5	36.0	34.5	33.0
E	Upper wing	15.3	13.8	12.3	16.8	15.3	13.8	18.3	16.8	15.3
G	Side seam	6.0	6.5	7.0	6.5	7.0	7.5	7.0	7.5	8.0
H	Neckline (excl. wire)	15.2	16.2	17.2	16.2	17.2	18.2	17.2	18.2	19.2
I	Across bust	13.9	15.1	16.3	15.1	16.3	17.5	16.3	17.5	18.7
J	Through bust	10.1	11.1	12.1	11.1	12.1	13.1	12.1	13.1	14.1
L	Under arm	8.5	9.0	9.5	9.0	9.5	10.0	9.5	10.0	10.5
M	Outer edge of wire casing	17.4	18.6	19.8	18.6	19.8	21.0	19.8	21.0	22.2
N	Centre front top width (incl.wires)	2.5	2.5	2.5	2.5	2.5	2.5	2.5	2.5	2.5
O	Centre front depth	3.7	3.7	3.7	3.7	3.7	3.7	3.7	3.7	3.7
P	Front strap length finished at	17.0	17.0	17.0	17.0	17.0	17.0	17.0	17.0	17.0
Q	Strap length cut	23.0	23.0	23.0	23.0	23.0	23.0	23.0	23.0	23.0
R	Adjustable length	11.0	11.0	11.0	11.0	11.0	11.0	11.0	11.0	11.0
S	Strap from back	4.5	5.0	5.5	4.0	4.5	5.0	3.5	4.0	4.5
	Wire play: 1cm									

Special Instructions:

NAME:	LVJ	DATE:	01/12/2014

As you can see from the spec sheet above, all 32 under-bands measure the same, and from 32A to 32C (increasing the cup size) the wing increases by 1.5cm. From the size 32C to 34C the wing also increase by 1.5cm (and the under-band by 5cm).

The Process

"Working out the wing measurements across the sizes when writing a spec sheet can be quite complicated when you start out. The easiest way is to work out each under-band group separately then move onto the next one.

I would then work out the 34 under-bands by using the base size 32C, knowing that the wing increases by 1.5cm to a 34C.

I can break it down. If the wing on a 32C measured 10cm then....

32C + wing grade = 34C
10cm + 1.5cm = 11.5cm

34C + wing grade = 34B
11.5cm + 1.5cm = 13cm

34B + wing grade = 34A
13cm + 1.5cm = 14.5cm

For example my base size was a 32C so I would work out the all the 32 bands, I would measure the wings, and knowing that they increase by 1.5cm, I could work out a size 32B, then increase again by 1.5cm to get a size 32A.

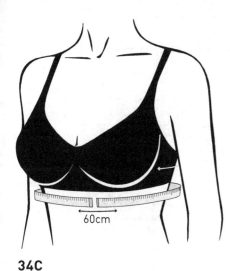

34C

34B

34A

It's sometimes easier to place your bra sizes in a grid table and work it out, then transfer that information into your spec sheet.

If 34B measured 60cm then 34A and 34C under-band would measure 60cm

You have now worked out all the 34 wing lengths

34A	34B	34C
14.5cm	13.0cm	11.5cm

Bottom of wing

Say the wing of a 32C is 10cm and I grade by 1.5cm. Then.....

32A = 12cm   32B = 11.5cm   32C = 10cm
34A = 14.5cm   34B = 12cm   34C = 11.5cm
36A = 16cm   36B = 14.5cm   36C = 13cm

DIFFERENCES WITH SHEETS

Different companies present their spec sheets in different ways; fundamentally they have the same information on though. It's just a personal preference. I have included three different lay outs of spec sheets for you to use, (permission is given to replicate these) just pick the one you think will suit you, and don't be afraid to change and improve it.

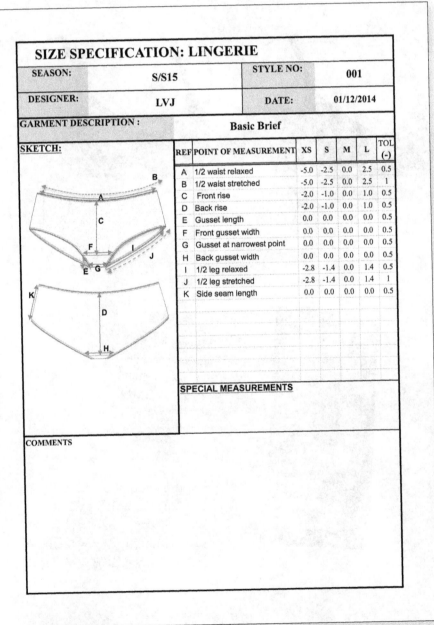

SPECIFICATION SHEET 2

SIZE SPECIFICATION		STYLE NO: 001	SUPPLIER: HOW TO BECOME A LINGERIE DESIGNER
GARMENT DESCRIPTION :	Basic Brief		

SKETCH:

REF	POINT OF MEASUREMENT		XS	S	M	L		TOL (-)
A	1/2 waist relaxed		-5.0	-2.5	0.0	2.5		0.5
B	1/2 waist stretched		-5.0	-2.5	0.0	2.5		1.0
C	Front rise		-2.0	-1.0	0.0	1.0		0.5
D	Back rise		-2.0	-1.0	0.0	1.0		0.5
E	Gusset length		0.0	0.0	0.0	0.0		0.5
F	Front gusset width		0.0	0.0	0.0	0.0		0.5
G	Gusset at narrowest point		0.0	0.0	0.0	0.0		0.5
H	Back gusset width		0.0	0.0	0.0	0.0		0.5
I	1/2 leg relaxed		-2.8	-1.4	0.0	1.4		0.5
J	1/2 leg stretched		-2.8	-1.4	0.0	1.4		1.0
K	Side seam length		0.0	0.0	0.0	0.0		0.5

Special Instructions:

NAME: LVJ   DATE: 01/12/2014

SPECIFICATION SHEET 3

SIZE SPECIFICATION

RANGE	
DATE	
STYLE NUMBER	
DESCRIPTION	

SKETCH:

REF	POINT OF MEASUREMENT	XS	S	M	L	TOL (-)
A	1/2 waist relaxed	-5.0	-2.5	0.0	2.5	0.5
B	1/2 waist stretched	-5.0	-2.5	0.0	2.5	1
C	Front rise	-2.0	-1.0	0.0	1.0	0.5
D	Back rise	-2.0	-1.0	0.0	1.0	0.5
E	Gusset length	0.0	0.0	0.0	0.0	0.5
F	Front gusset width	0.0	0.0	0.0	0.0	0.5
G	Gusset at narrowest point	0.0	0.0	0.0	0.0	0.5
H	Back gusset width	0.0	0.0	0.0	0.0	0.5
I	1/2 leg relaxed	-2.8	-1.4	0.0	1.4	0.5
J	1/2 leg stretched	-2.8	-1.4	0.0	1.4	1
K	Side seam length	0.0	0.0	0.0	0.0	0.5

SPECIAL INSTRUCTIONS:

BLANK VERSIONS OF THE **SHEETS** FOR YOUR USE

BLANK SPECIFICATION SHEET 1

SIZE SPECIFICATION: LINGERIE						
SEASON:			**STYLE NO:**			
DESIGNER:			**DATE:**			
GARMENT DESCRIPTION :		Basic Brief				

SKETCH:	REF	POINT OF MEASUREMENT	XS	S	M	L	TOL (-)
	SPECIAL MEASUREMENTS						

COMMENTS

SIZE SPECIFICATION		STYLE NO:	SUPPLIER:
GARMENT DESCRIPTION :			

SKETCH:	REF	POINT OF MEASUREMENT	XS	S	M	L		TOL (-)

Special Instructions:

NAME:	DATE:

SIZE SPECIFICATION

RANGE	
DATE	
STYLE NUMBER	
DESCRIPTION	

SKETCH:

REF	POINT OF MEASUREMENT	XS	S	M	L	TOL (-)

SPECIAL INSTRUCTIONS:

CHAPTER 3

HOW TO GRADE A BRA & BRIEF

INTRODUCTION

Whether you're a designer starting out in your career and want to know more about grading? An individual who wants to start their own lingerie label or a home sewer who just wants to understand and grade a lingerie pattern. This book will take you through step-by-step, from the beginning sharing industry standard grade information.

It will provide you with diagrams where and how to grade your lingerie pattern, examples of grading different lingerie briefs, and examples of grading underwired and non-wired bras.

By the end of this book you will understand the basic fundamental process of grading, with the last grades set out for you to complete.

I AM ALWAYS DOING THAT WHICH I CANNOT DO, IN ORDER THAT I MAY LEARN HOW TO DO IT

PABLO PICASSO

WHAT IS GRADING?

The term pattern grading, may evoke the impression of dealing with complicated measurements and fancy rulers or equipment. The reality though once the process is learnt, grading is straight forward.

Meaning that as an independent designer you can do just as good a job as the big fashion houses.

Grading started in the 1970s when pattern sales were dropping and patterns began to be made in multiple sizes. To start with a block pattern is drafted (in one size), then once fit is approved, it is graded (increased or decreased geometrically.

This process of resizing the base pattern is called "grading". For example, a base size 10 pattern will be made bigger to produce a size 12 and made smaller to produce a size 8.

The purpose of grading patterns is to increase or decrease the size of the pattern as per the grading rules, whilst retaining the shape, fit and scale of the garment proportionally to that of the original master pattern. It's important to remember that grading only makes a pattern larger or smaller and isn't intended to change the shape.

Pattern companies and manufacturers usually take the middle size of the pattern and grade it up for the larger sizes and down for the smaller sizes. This can only be done two or three times before the pattern becomes distorted.
If you were to have a range of 28A going up to 36D that alone is a total of 20 different sizes therefore 20 patterns pieces for each part. So usually cup sizes are graded individually i.e. 30B, 32B, 34B, 36B then C Cups D cups etc.

"There are three basic methods of grading: cut and spread, pattern shifting and computer grading. No one method is technically superior and all are equally capable of producing a correct grade."

CUT AND SPREAD

This book will be looking at the industry's standard grading rules where you will note that grading doesn't make everything equally larger or smaller. Different body parts increase at different proportional amounts. For example, the width of a pattern increases more than the height of the pattern between sizes.

Measurements are pre-determined by the company you are working for. Each company determines its own grade specifications for each size, and size specifications vary from manufacturer to manufacturer.

The pattern is cut across the full width of the pattern at different points and then the pieces are spread out by a specific amount to grade up. To grade down instead of spreading the pattern out the pattern is overlapped. No special training or tools are required; just scissors, a pencil, tape and a ruler. This method is good if you are altering patterns to fit your shape i.e. a bought vintage pattern now needed to fit the modern-day body. You can increase different parts of the pattern by different amounts and see an overall view. If you using this method, try to avoid cutting through darts or pleats.

PATTERN SHIFTING

This is the process of increasing the overall dimensions of a pattern, by moving it a measured distance up and down; and a measured distance left and right. Then the outline is re-drawn.
This will produce the same results as the cut-and-spread method, but you don't have to worry about the time-consuming approach of cutting up your pattern or knowing where to cut.

Pattern shifting is the method that we are using in this book.

COMPUTER GRADING

This is the fastest method of grading. Computer grading allows more options, by grading a line, and angles, rather than relying on grading on the X and Y-axis as the pattern shifting does. Today most manufacturers grade patterns on CAD systems.

To begin, the pattern maker guides a cursor around the edges of the sample pattern, on a digitized table. At each of the key points, he or she pushes a button to record a grade point.
(Which may be a corner, curve point or notch).

Each point is cross-referenced by a grade-rule table stored in the computer. If the pattern was originally made on the computer; the data will already be there and the pattern will enlarge or reduce automatically.
Once the pattern is in the system, a grade-rule table can be assigned to it and it will either grade the pattern automatically; or grade rules can be applied to each point of the pattern individually. The computerized plotter can then print out the patterns in every size.
Although many small firms still use traditional grading methods. Grading, like patternmaking, is becoming increasingly computerized.

STANDARD GRADES FOR BRIEFS

As mentioned, the middle size pattern is used for grading; the pattern is drafted and then graded up and down. Grading can only jump two or three sizes at a time before the pattern shape distorts.

"Grade rules depend on the garment. Each company will work to their own grading system. Most high-street companies that I have worked for use the basic grading system, which is what this book will look at. However, some companies tweak their grades, for example the side seam or gusset seam can grade at 0.5cm on bigger sizes, to allow for the change in the body shape".

You need your spec sheet or knowledge of how much you are grading by before you grade, this information tells you how much to increase or decrease the pattern by to get the other sizes.

A full look at spec sheets can be found in the book "How to spec a bra and brief"

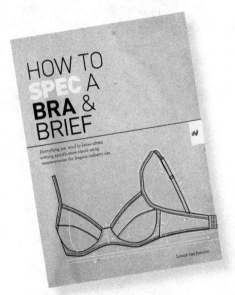

"Some textbooks say that you should grade the height of a brief depending where the crotch seam is — for example if the crotch seam is located towards the back, then most of the grade should go on the front and less on the back. I have never done this and so for simplicity I will keep the front and back grade the same."

The measurements in this book are typical of industry standard grades and are as follows:

MEASUREMENTS TO INCREASE OR DECREASE WHEN GRADING A BRIEF

- A ½ Waist Relaxed: 2.5cm
- B ½ Waist Extended: 2.5cm
- C Front Rise: 1cm
- D Back Rise: 1cm
- E Gusset Length: 0cm
- F Front Gusset Width: 0cm
- G Back Gusset Width: 0cm
- H Side Seam Length: 0cm
- I ½ Leg Relaxed: 1.4cm
- J ½ Leg Extended: 1.4cm

Some companies grade briefs, by splitting the grade on the pattern, for example as the brief height increases by 1cm they would move the brief up by 0.5cm and move the brief down by 0.5cm to gain the 1cm increase. Again, to keep things simple, we are going to put all the grade on one side of the brief. It's a lot easier to notice mistakes doing it this way.

When grading the brief, if the left and right side of the pattern is the same, (it usually is unless you have an asymmetrical style line) you only need to grade one side of a pattern then mirror it.

"Please note, to keep it simple the grade shall just state 'increase' when in fact to go down a size the operation will be reversed and the grade decreased. It just saves having to read (and write) increase/decrease continuously.

So in all places where it states increasing the grade, to gain a smaller size everything need to be done in reverse. E.g. if you increase the height by 1cm to gain a bigger size, to gain a smaller size you need to decrease the height by 1cm.

Note also that, if you've drawn a line 1cm above the guide line to increase the size then you will need to draw a line 1cm below the guide line to decrease the size of the pattern down."

GRADING
A FULL
BRIEF

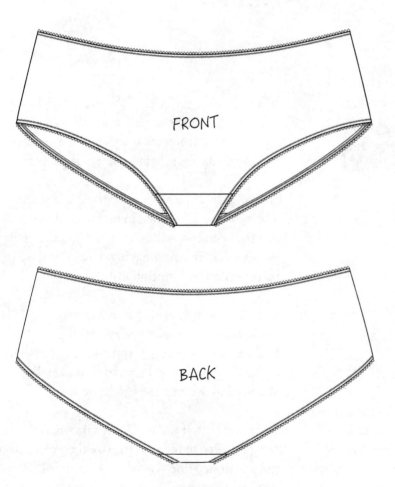

GRADING THE FRONT

The first brief to be graded is a basic hipster style brief. It comprises of a front piece, a back piece and a gusset.

The following steps are what you will be following for all the grading – each new style will state how much you will need to grade the pattern by.

For every pattern the principles will stay the same, drawing around your pattern piece and marking in the cross and drawing in the guide and grade lines.

First you need to note at each point of the pattern how much the brief increases by, for the grade. (see step 1)

Fig 1

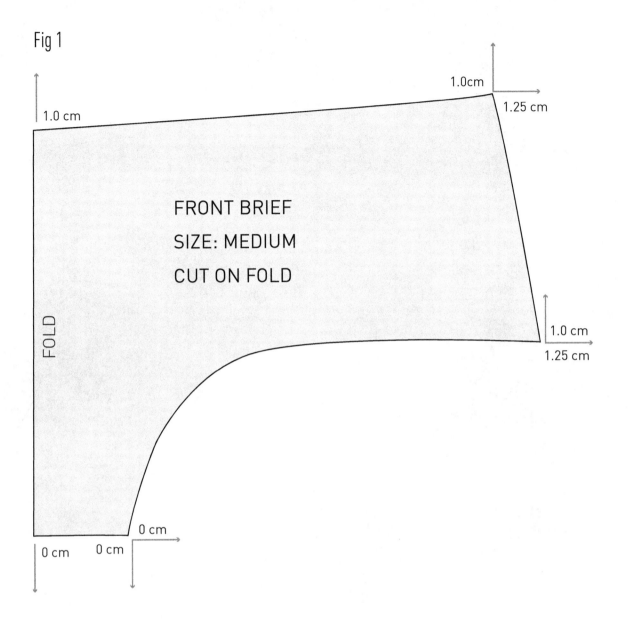

STEP 1
MARKING WHERE THE GRADE GOES
SEE Fig 1

You know that the front and back rise of the brief increases by 1 cm vertically and increases on the half by 1.25cm. So firstly, you need to work out where the grade goes.

At each point of the pattern there will a grade direction in which the brief will move.

Start at the Centre Front and go around clockwise marking each point. By doing this you can ensure you have covered every point.

Knowing that the front rise increases by 1cm, at the Centre Front the grade direction (to increase a size) will be an arrow pointing upwards with the amount 1cm. As this is on the fold and will be mirrored the grade cannot go in any other direction.

The next point that is to be graded is the top of the side seam/waist (going clockwise), we know that the front rise increases by 1cm so like the previous point, an arrow will be pointing upwards (increasing the grade) with the amount 1cm.

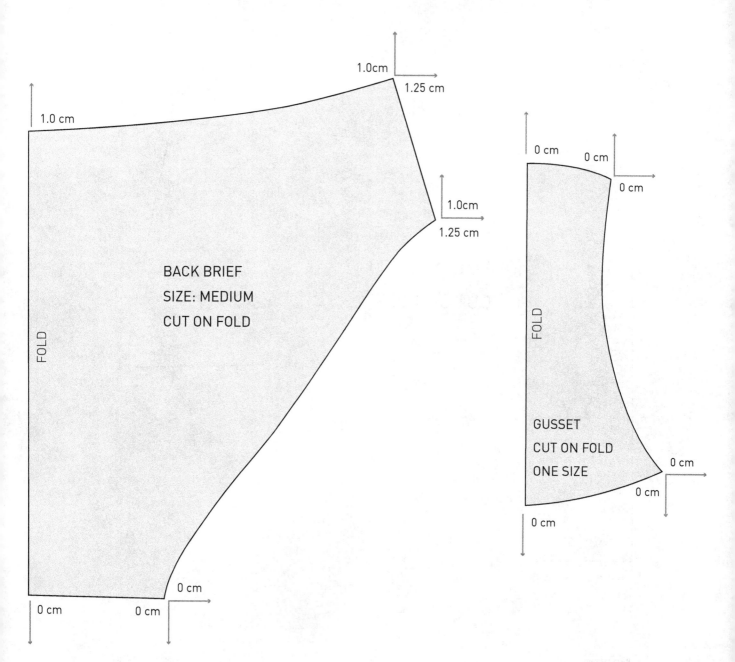

We also know that on the half, that the brief increases by 1.25cm, an arrow will point right (to increase) with the amount 1.25cm.

The next point is the lower point of the side seam/leg. As we are not going to increase the depth of the side seam, the measurements need to follow the previous measurements. This point will go up 1cm if you didn't put this point up by 1cm what would happen is that the side seam would increase by 1cm at each grade, and the leg curve would stay the same on a size XS and XL which would be incorrect.

The point also needs to moved out by 1.25cm to allow for the increase of width.

The next point of the pattern is the leg/gusset, as you have added all the height increase in the front pattern of the brief and you are not going to increase the gusset piece. A zero is written on both arrows going down and out. It's important when starting out to mark when there will be no increase, so by looking back you know exactly how it will be graded.

The next point is the gusset on the fold, again as there is no increase a zero is written down. The back pattern gets graded the same as the front so the measurement markings will be the same.

Fig 2

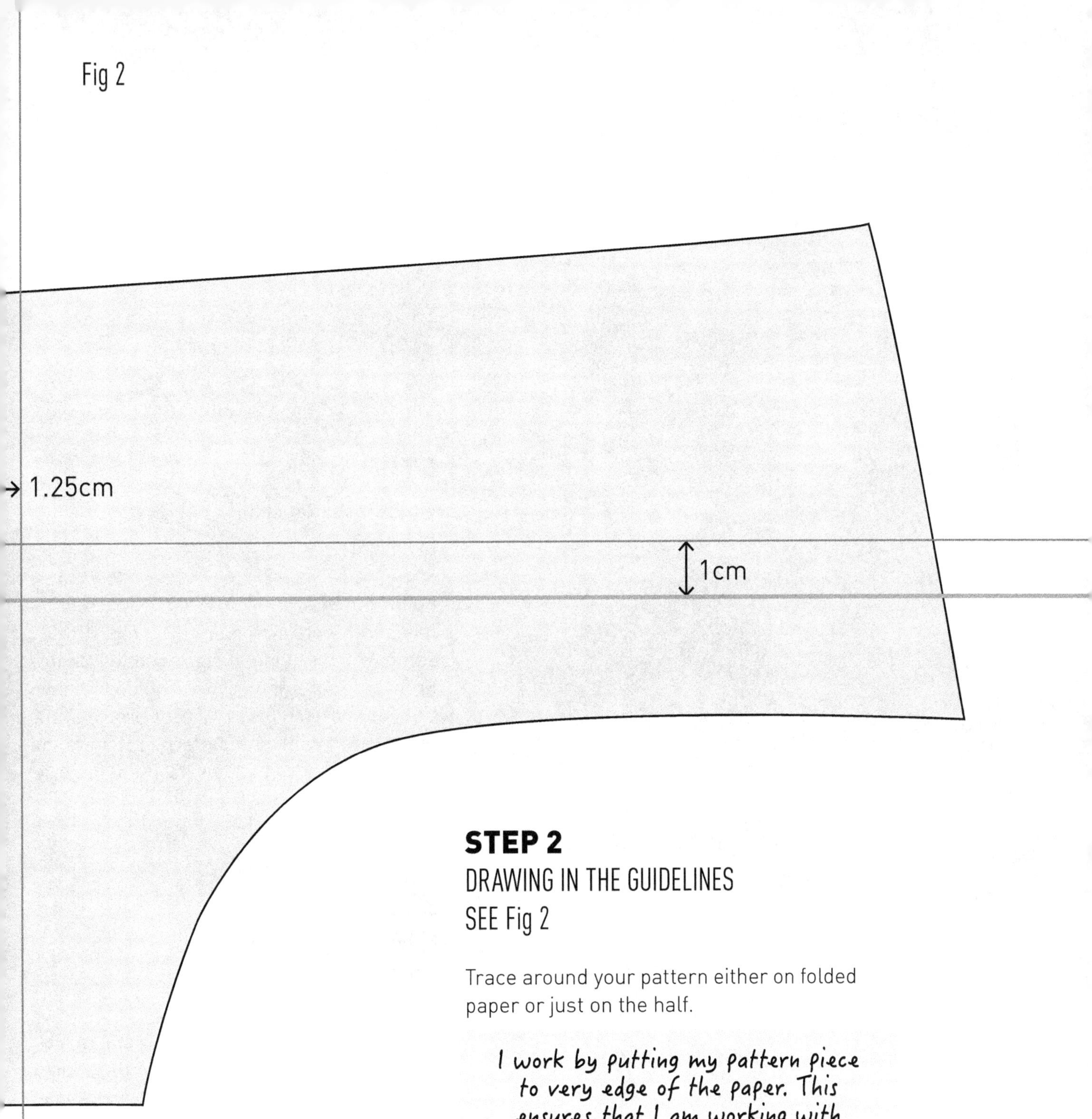

→ 1.25cm

↕ 1cm

STEP 2
DRAWING IN THE GUIDELINES
SEE Fig 2

Trace around your pattern either on folded paper or just on the half.

I work by putting my pattern piece to very edge of the paper. This ensures that I am working with a straight line and eliminates the need to check that line.

Remove pattern. Draw a horizontal line across the paper, re-lay your pattern over your traced pattern and draw in the horizontal line over the pattern so they match. This is your guide line as well as the edge of the paper.

On the piece of paper that you traced your pattern on, with a different colour draw a vertical line 1.25cm away from the edge of the pattern (CF). Then draw another horizontal line 1cm up from the first guide line you have drawn.

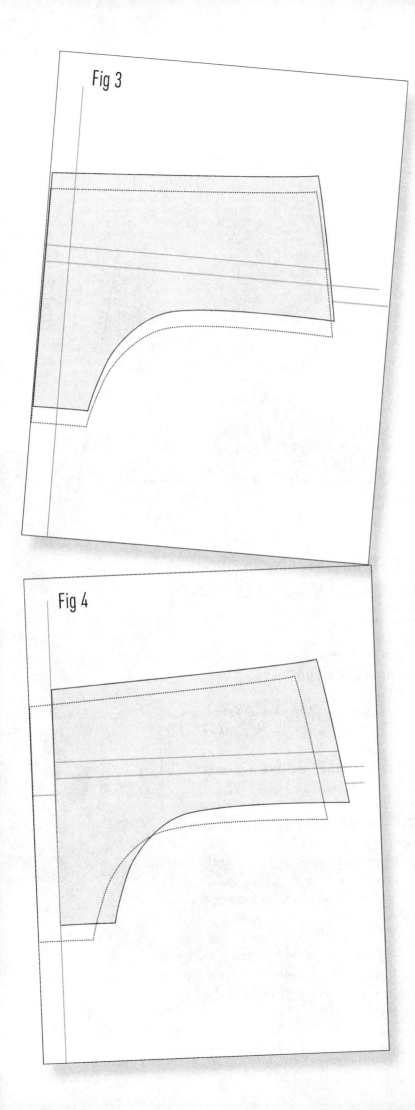

STEP 3
MOVING THE BRIEF UP
SEE Fig 3

Following the same order that you wrote the measurements in, the brief will move the same. We are going to start with the Centre Front measurement, so moving up by 1cm. Lay your pattern on top of your drawn around pattern and shift your pattern up 1cm to the new line. Draw in the new height of the brief at the Centre Front.

STEP 4
MOVING THE BRIEF OUT
SEE Fig 4

Now whilst you have the pattern shifted up, shift your pattern out 1.25cm, so the edge of the pattern is in line with the drawn vertical line. Draw across the top of the brief joining up with the line you have just drawn. Continue around the side seam and down into the leg to the gusset seam.

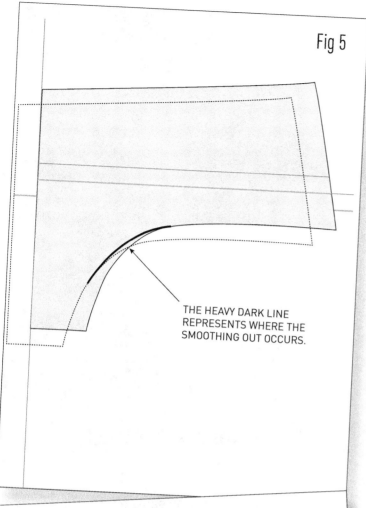

Fig 5

THE HEAVY DARK LINE REPRESENTS WHERE THE SMOOTHING OUT OCCURS.

STEP 5
SMOOTHING OUT THE LEG
SEE Fig 5

As the gusset area does not grade in width top or bottom, you need to re-draw in the leg opening to join the new pattern with the old pattern. This is done by blending the new front leg line into the old gusset line, ensuring that the leg-opening curve is maintained. This should be a smooth curve line.

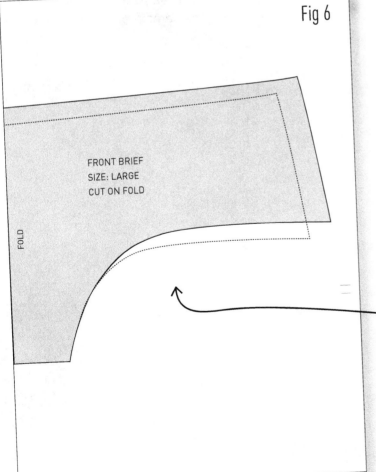

Fig 6

FRONT BRIEF
SIZE: LARGE
CUT ON FOLD

SEE Fig 6
This is what it looks like when the new and old patterns sit together.

Fig 7

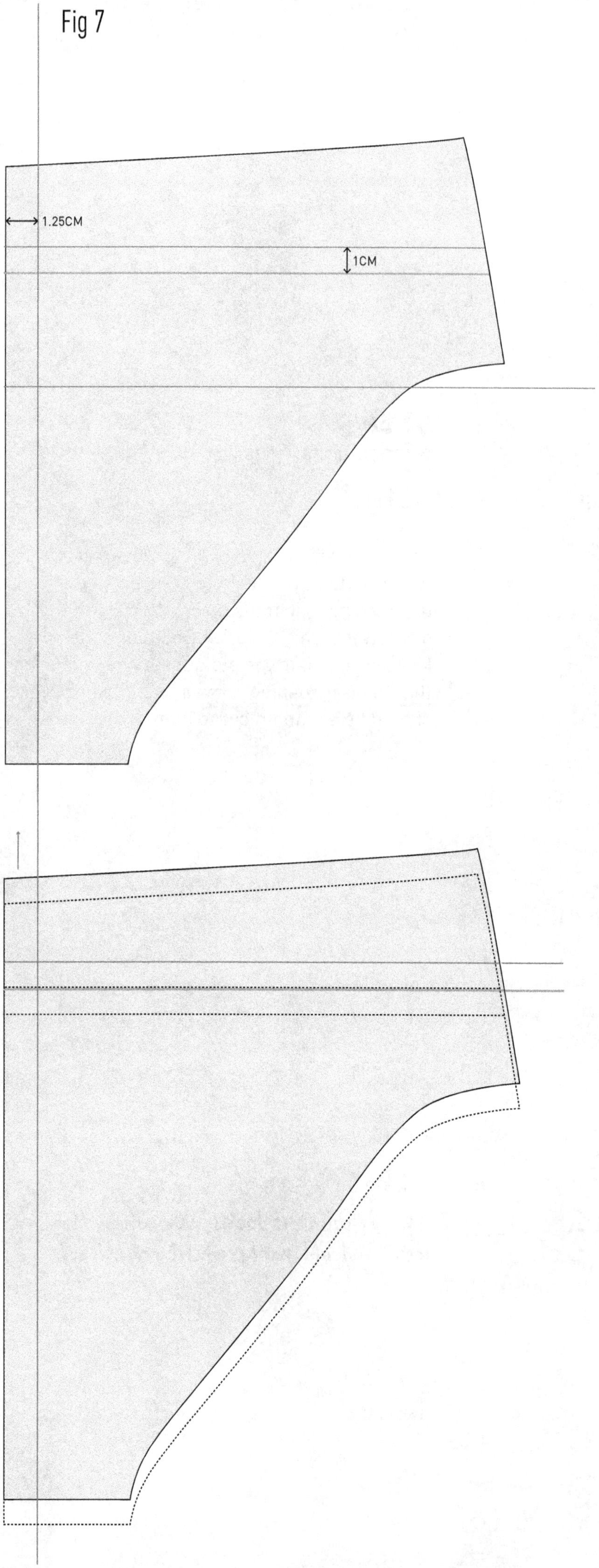

1.25CM

1CM

GRADING THE BACK
SEE Fig 7

This grades the same as the front.
Following the same method as in steps 1-4.

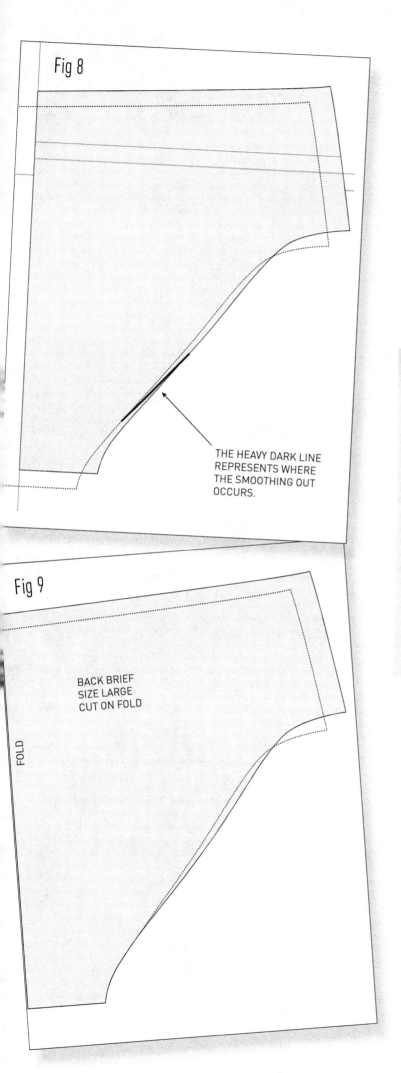

Fig 8

THE HEAVY DARK LINE REPRESENTS WHERE THE SMOOTHING OUT OCCURS.

Fig 9

BACK BRIEF
SIZE LARGE
CUT ON FOLD

STEP 6
MOVING THE GRADE UP AND OUT
SEE Fig 8

Blend new leg line into the old leg line near the gusset ensuring that the back-leg curve is smooth.

This is what it looks like when the new and old patterns sit together. SEE Fig 9

Note*
By moving the leg out by 1.25cm, it looks like you're under by 0.15cm, however due to the curve of the front and back leg, and that you have increased the rise by 1cm that 0.15cm evens itself out. You also have the elastic application, so if for some reason the shape of your brief isn't grading by 1.4cm and only 1.3cm then the elastic application can take it to 1.4cm.

STEP 7
GRADING THE GUSSET PIECE
SEE Fig 10

The Spec indicates that the gusset doesn't grade in any direction, width or height, so the same pattern piece is used for all the sizes.

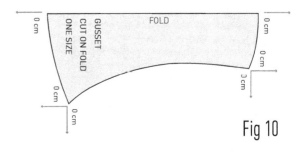

Fig 10

GRADING A HIGH WAISTED BRIEF

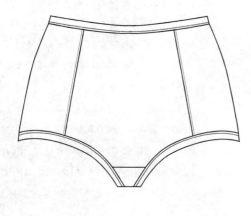

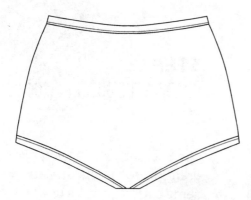

The next brief to be graded is a high-waisted brief, with a centre front panel and side panel. Technically the same grade rules apply to this style as the one previous. However, because there are more pieces you must decide how and where to split the grade.

Unless there is extra information on your spec sheet where the grade needs to go, you split the grade equally between the front and side panel or as close to it as possible.

So instead of the whole front panel increasing by 1.25 (on the half), the Centre front panel will increase by 0.65cm and the side panel by 0.6cm. These grades are not set in stone, so after a size range is made; you will be able to see if the grade needs tweaking. The back has only one panel so will be the same grade as the previous brief. The side seam, doesn't increase so you don't need to increase the side panel front depth.

Fig 1

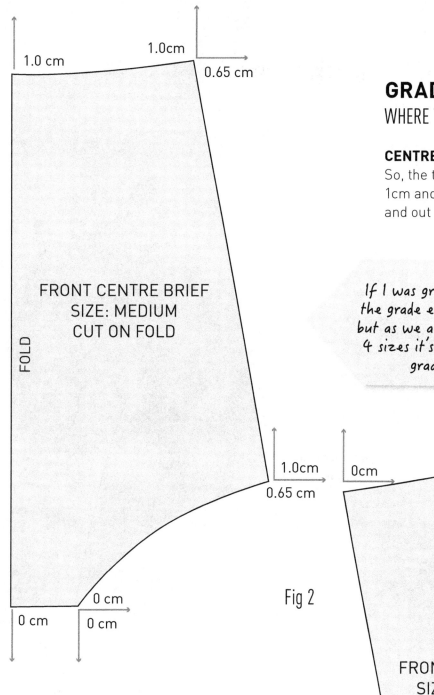

Fig 2

GRADING
WHERE THE GRADE GOES

CENTRE FRONT SEE Fig 1
So, the top of the centre front, increases by 1cm and the next two points raises up by 1cm and out by 0.65cm

If I was grading by computer I would split the grade exact and grade would be 0.625, but as we are grading manually a brief over 4 sizes it's not detrimental that one piece grade 0.05 mm difference.

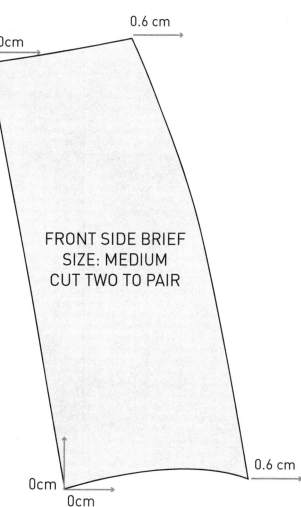

SIDE FRONT SEE Fig 2
The side seam, doesn't grade (so isn't increasing), and the side which is being sewn to the front doesn't grade, (otherwise this will distort the waist curve). It's only the points by the side seam that grade out by 06.cm.

GUSSET PIECE SEE Fig 3

The gusset piece doesn't grade so nothing should be done on this piece.

BACK PIECE SEE Fig 4

The back gets graded with the full grade as it is one piece, so will grade 1cm up and 1.25cm across like the previous brief.

Fig 3

Fig 4

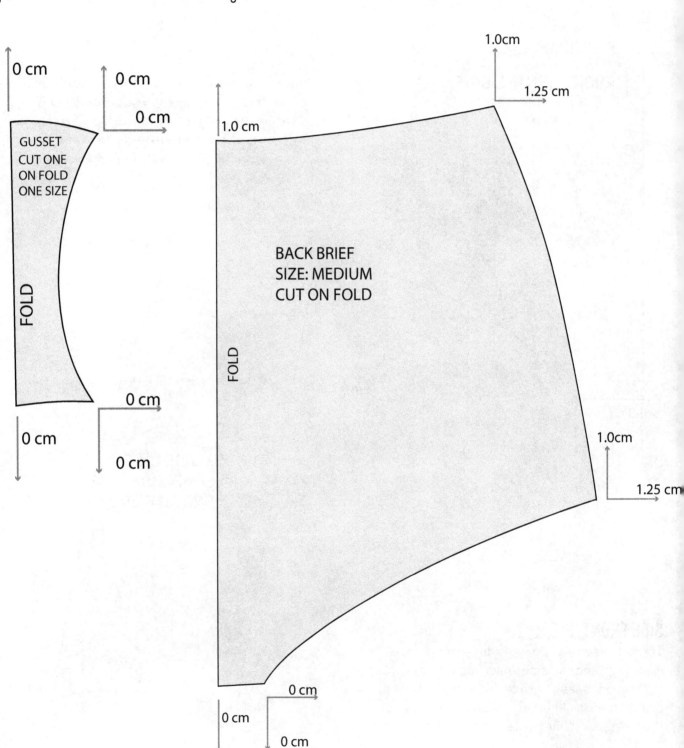

Fig 5

0.65CM

1CM

GRADING STEPS OF FRONT BRIEF

MOVING THE PATTERN UP
SEE Fig 5

Draw in the guidelines, then shift your pattern up by 1cm, marking the new top pattern line, and then shift your pattern out 0.65 cm.

Draw around the front side seam and down into the gusset.

Fig 6

SMOOTHING THE LEG
SEE Fig 6

No lines cross at the gusset area on this pattern so you just need to extend the leg curve into the old curve.

THE HEAVY DARK LINE REPRESENTS WHERE THE LINE EXTENDS INTO THE ORIGINAL GUSSET.

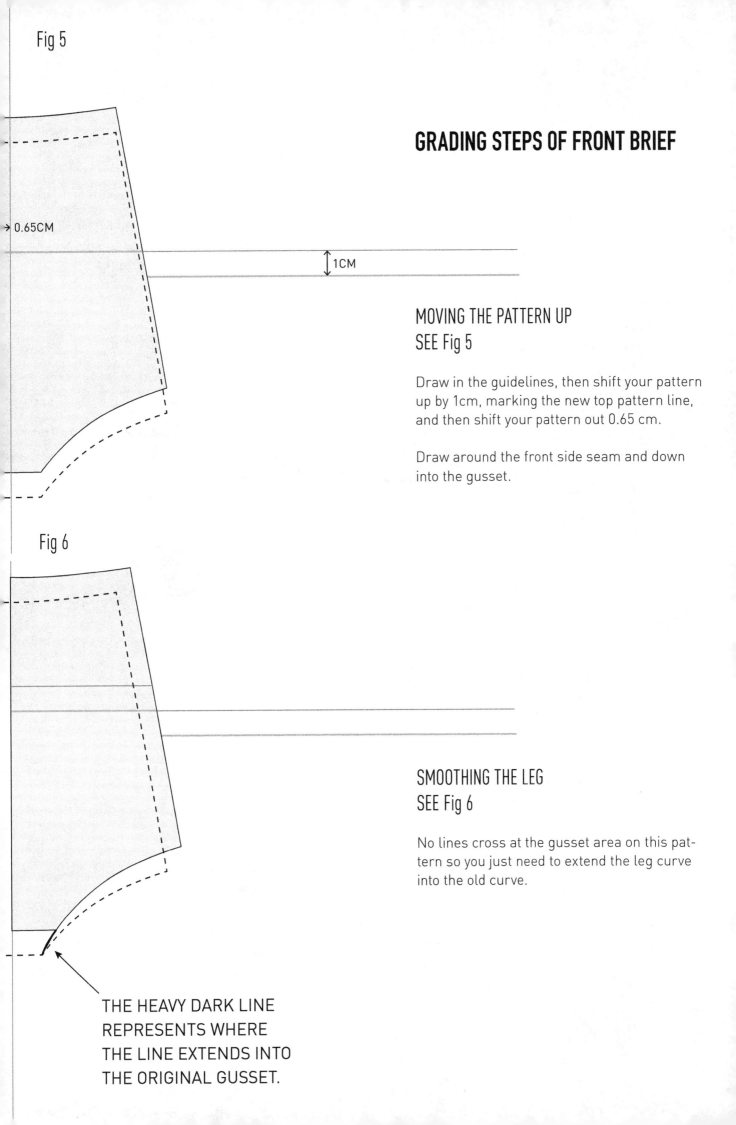

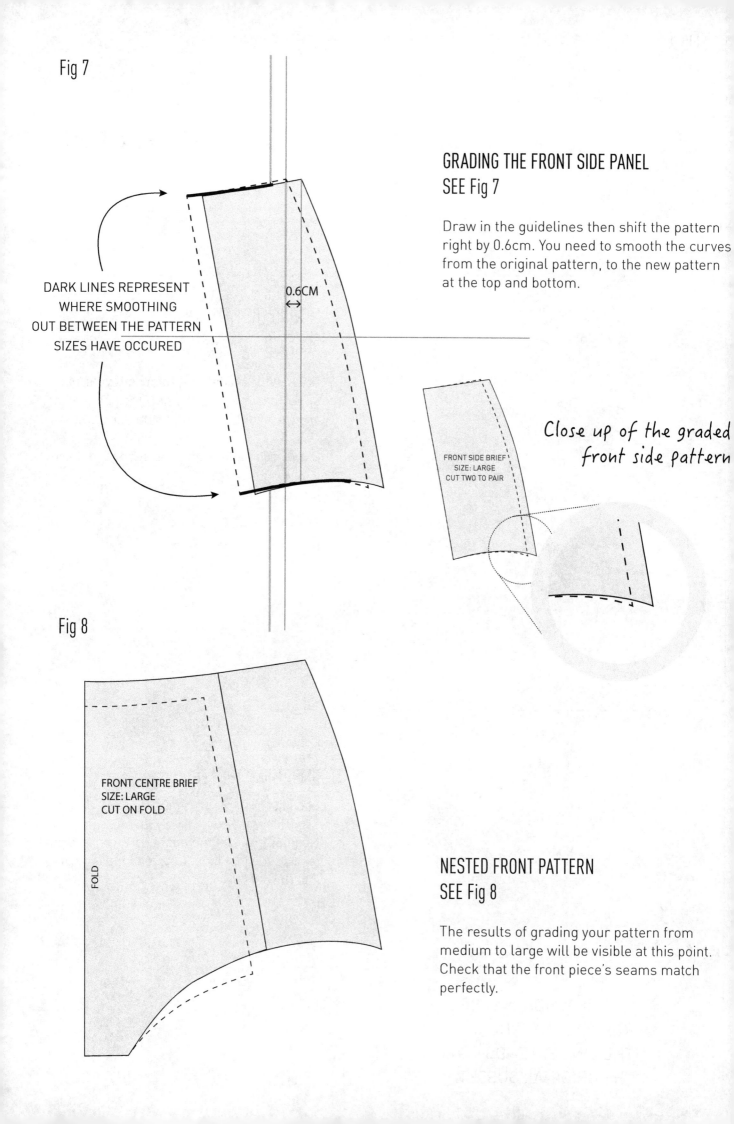

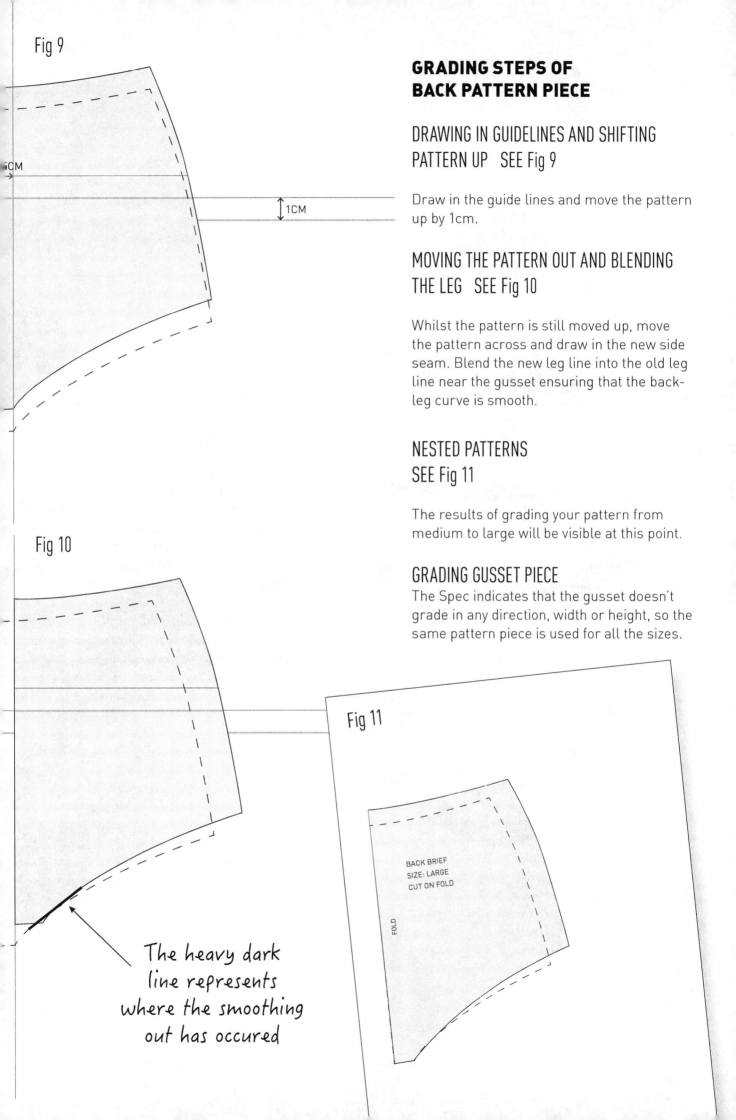

GRADING STEPS OF BACK PATTERN PIECE

DRAWING IN GUIDELINES AND SHIFTING PATTERN UP   SEE Fig 9

Draw in the guide lines and move the pattern up by 1cm.

MOVING THE PATTERN OUT AND BLENDING THE LEG   SEE Fig 10

Whilst the pattern is still moved up, move the pattern across and draw in the new side seam. Blend the new leg line into the old leg line near the gusset ensuring that the back-leg curve is smooth.

NESTED PATTERNS
SEE Fig 11

The results of grading your pattern from medium to large will be visible at this point.

GRADING GUSSET PIECE
The Spec indicates that the gusset doesn't grade in any direction, width or height, so the same pattern piece is used for all the sizes.

The heavy dark line represents where the smoothing out has occured

GRADING A LACE STYLE BACK BRIEF

This style of brief has a plain front and galloon lace on the lower back. What differs on this pattern is that there is a centre seam on the back, please don't be thrown by the fact that you are going to grade scallop lace. Just be aware of the angle of which the triangle at the top of the Centre back sits into the lace.

As per the previous briefs the width on the half grade by 1.25cm, so to keep the angles the same at the back; the pattern points of that angle on both pieces need to grade the same. This ensures that the briefs fit together on the larger and smaller sizes with ease.

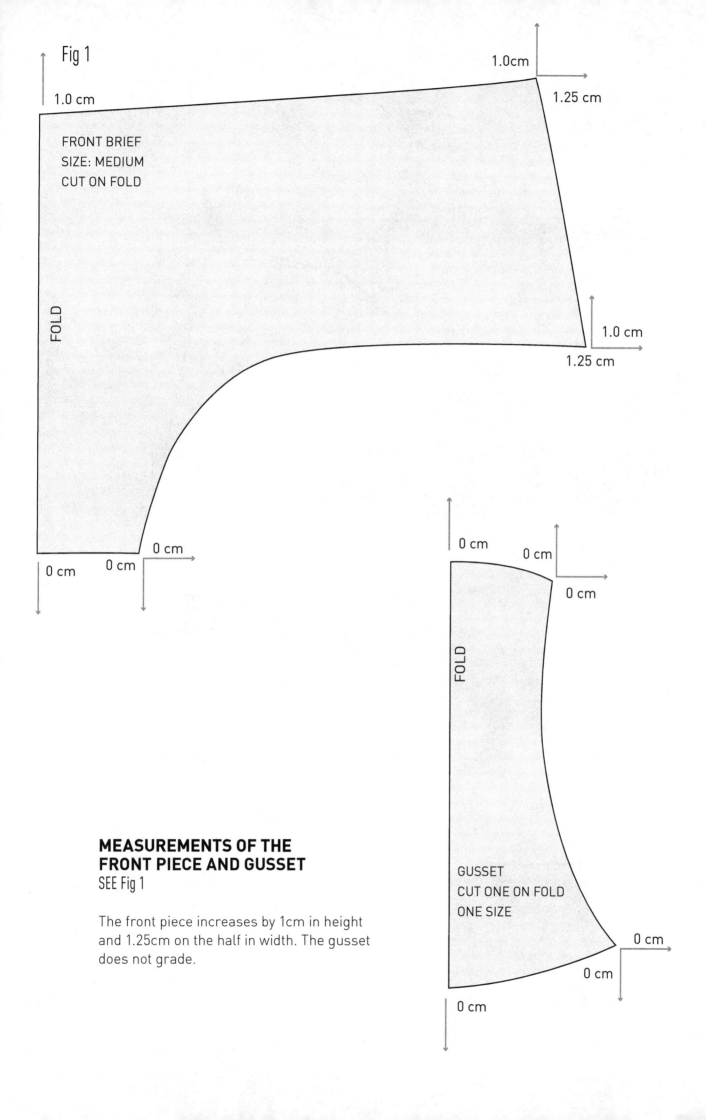

Fig 1

FRONT BRIEF
SIZE: MEDIUM
CUT ON FOLD

FOLD

GUSSET
CUT ONE ON FOLD
ONE SIZE

**MEASUREMENTS OF THE
FRONT PIECE AND GUSSET**
SEE Fig 1

The front piece increases by 1cm in height and 1.25cm on the half in width. The gusset does not grade.

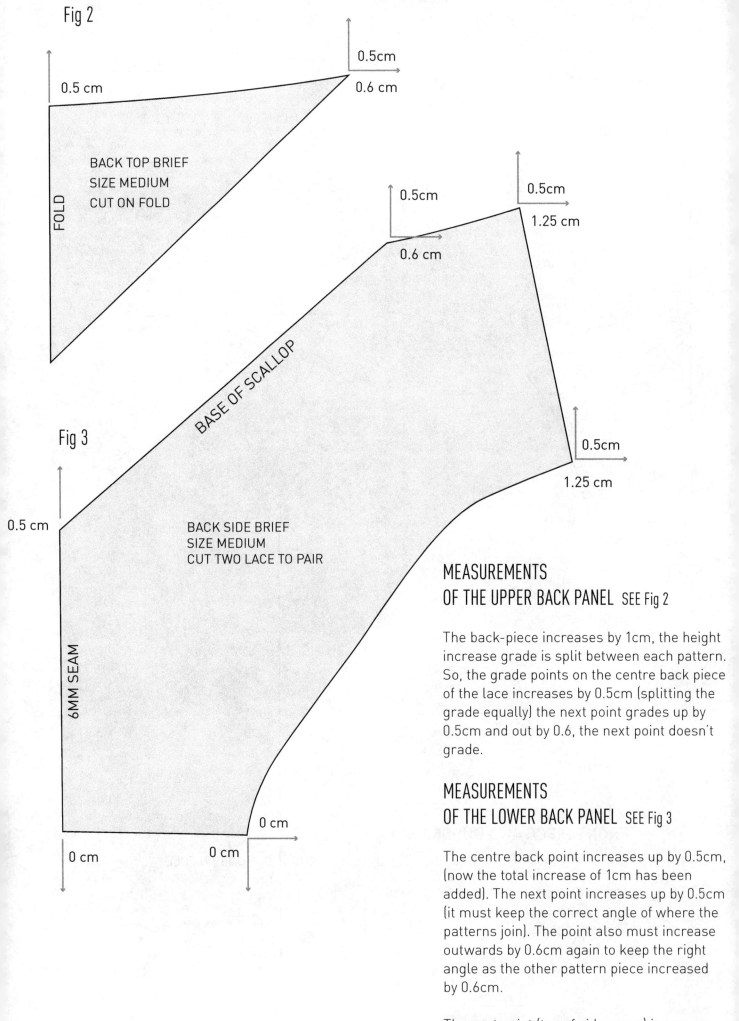

MEASUREMENTS OF THE UPPER BACK PANEL SEE Fig 2

The back-piece increases by 1cm, the height increase grade is split between each pattern. So, the grade points on the centre back piece of the lace increases by 0.5cm (splitting the grade equally) the next point grades up by 0.5cm and out by 0.6, the next point doesn't grade.

MEASUREMENTS OF THE LOWER BACK PANEL SEE Fig 3

The centre back point increases up by 0.5cm, (now the total increase of 1cm has been added). The next point increases up by 0.5cm (it must keep the correct angle of where the patterns join). The point also must increase outwards by 0.6cm again to keep the right angle as the other pattern piece increased by 0.6cm.

The next point (top of side seam) increases height by 0.5cm and it increases out by 1.25.

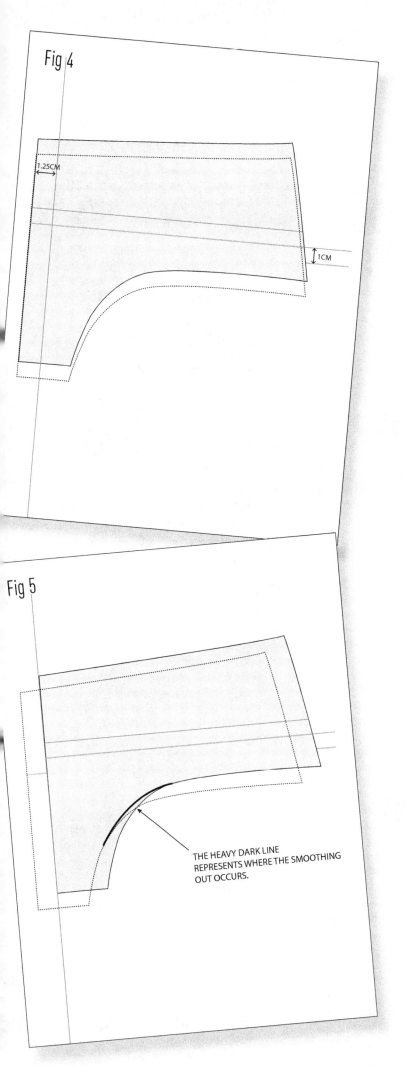

This measurement must be 1.25cm for two reasons:

1. We have split the grade, so the centre back piece has increased by 0.6cm so we only need to add 0.65cm across the waist on the lower brief pattern. We have already moved 0.6 on the second point, so if we increased the next point by 0.65 then the waist measurement will only be increasing by 0.5. The larger pattern piece needs to move out 1.25cm

eg.(1.25-0.6=0.65cm)

2. The lower point of the seam needs to move out 1.25cm to increase grade as there is no split grade across this section of the pattern. And because this needs to move out 1.25cm then the previous point needs to as well to keep the side seam angle correct.

GRADING THE FRONT PANEL

MOVING THE BRIEF UP SEE Fig 4

Move the brief up 1cm and draw in a new top line

MOVING THE BRIEF OUT AND BLENDING THE LEG SEE Fig 5

After moving the front panel up and out, blend the new leg line into the old leg line near the gusset ensuring that the front-leg curve is smooth.

THE HEAVY DARK LINE REPRESENTS WHERE THE SMOOTHING OUT OCCURS.

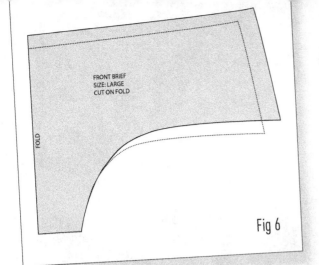

NESTED PATTERNS SEE Fig 6

Check the patterns against each other. This is what it looks like when the new and old patterns sit together.

GRADING THE BACK PANEL

MARKING GUIDELINES AND MOVING THE BRIEF UP SEE Fig 7

Move the centre back up by 0.5cm

MOVING THE BRIEF OUT SEE Fig 8

Whilst the pattern has been shifted up, shift it out 0.6cm. Mark in new top inner seam. The Centre back top panel is added in a dashed line to check the angles are okay and so you can see how the patterns sit together.

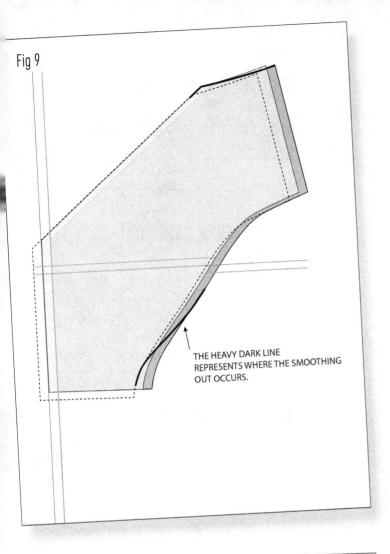

SMOOTHING THE LINES SEE Fig 9

This image shows the dashed line which was the original pattern piece, the light grey which was the shift of 0.6cm and the dark grey which is the shift of 1.25cm.

The dark lines represent the smoothing out of the top of the waist to the angle. The new leg line blends into the old leg line near the gusset ensuring that the back-leg curve is smooth.

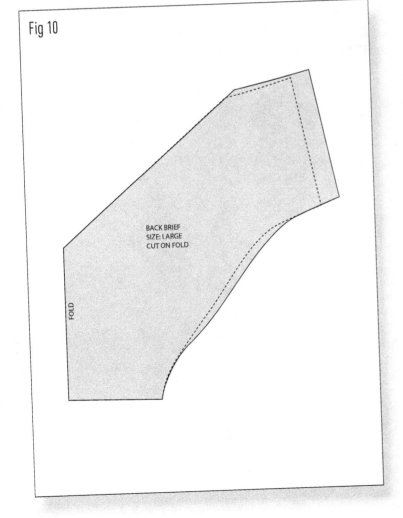

NESTED PATTERNS SEE Fig 10

Check the patterns against each other. This is what it looks like when the new and old patterns sit together.

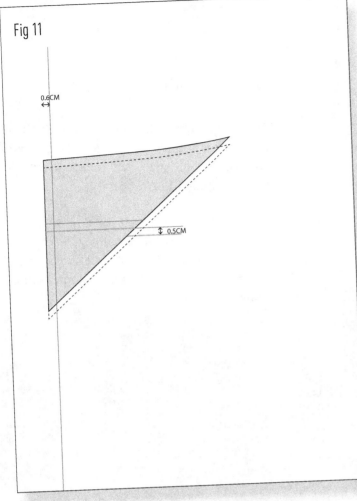

Fig 11

GRADING CENTRE BACK PANEL

SHIFTING THE CENTRE BACK PANEL UP
SEE Fig 11

Shift the pattern up by 0.5cm

SHIFTING THE PATTERN OUT
SEE Fig 12

Whilst the pattern is shifted up, move the pattern out 0.6cm. Draw across the top of the triangle pattern and down the side. There are no lines crossing so you don't have to smooth any out.

NESTED PATTERNS SEE FIG 13

This is what it looks like when the new and old patterns sit together.

GRADING GUSSET PIECE

The Spec indicates that the gusset doesn't grade in any direction, width or height, so the same pattern piece is used for all the sizes.

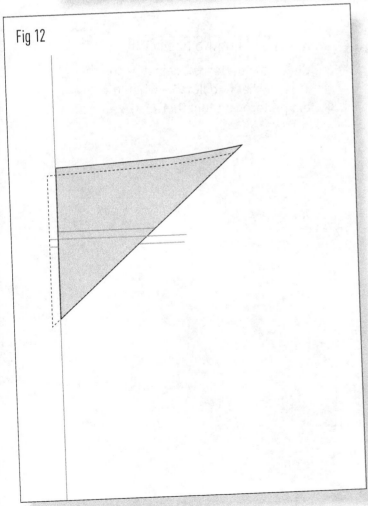

Fig 12

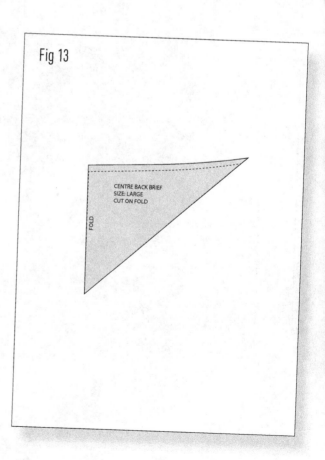

Fig 13

STANDARD GRADE FOR A

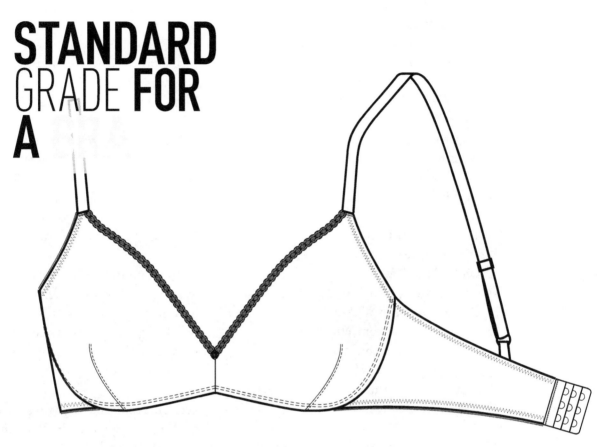

Before starting to grade your bra, you need to look at your spec sheet or the given measurements before you grade. This will confirm how much you need to increase or decrease the pattern by to achieve the other sizes.

As with the briefs this book uses industry standard grades that are used in the UK, (the UK underband grades by 5cm whereas a typical French brand grades by 4cm). These are some of the measurements that are used on a basic soft bra grading rules that can be used as a starting point, or as your actual grade.

A full insight into writing specification sheets can be found in the book "How to spec a bra & brief" which covers the different amounts of grade that can occur at each point of measurement."

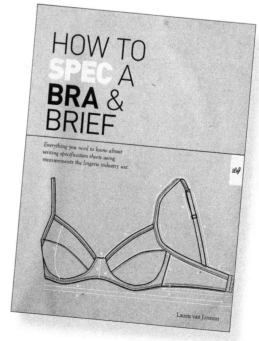

They are for sizes x/small – x/large.

A Under-bust Relaxed: 5.0cm
B Under-bust Extended: 5.0cm
C Lower Wing Relaxed: 1.5cm
D Lower Wing Extended: 1.5cm
E Upper Wing: 1.5cm
F Wing to Cup: 0.5cm
G Side Seam: 0.5cm
H Neckline: 1.0cm
I Across Bust: 1.0cm
J Through Bust: 1.0cm
K Dart Length: 0.5cm
L Under Arm: 0.5cm
M Outer Edge of Wire Casing: N/A
N Centre Front Top Width: 0cm
O Centre Front Bottom Width: 0.cm
P Centre Front Depth: 0cm
Q Strap Length Cut: N/A
R Adjustable Length: N/A
S Strap from Centre Back: 0.5cm

When grading an under-wire bra, the grade will differ depending on the grade of the wire. The grade of the wire can differ usually from 1.2cm to 2.3cm, which will in turn alter the 'across and through bust' measurement.

"When we come to underwire bras we will look at grading sizes 32A up to 36C and will be cross grading. Grading across band and cup sizes can differ depending on the style and company you work for; we will use the same grade for the underwire bra as the soft bra but also insert the measurement 'M' Outer Edge of Wire Casing."

GRADING A BRA

If you have read any of the other books, you will note that cross-grading pops up quite a bit. So, for those you haven't read about it, here goes....

When grading it's important to remember that the cup size and band size work together, i.e. the wearer of a 32C cup has a smaller bust than a 34C cup wearer. The wearer of a 36B is wearing the same cup capacity as someone wearing a 32D. Confused? You're not the only one.

Without understanding this knowledge someone wearing a 34B who thought they needed a bigger band may just go buy a 36B but this would mean they had gone up a band size and a cup size, and it's by this, that causes many women confusion and wear the wrong size bra.

Welcome to the cross-grading system. Cross grading a bra is when a 34B has the same cup size as a 32C and 30D, however the 32C has a smaller back. Woman are usually wearing the right cup size, but a too bigger back which is why the back of the bra rises. By going down a band size and up a cup size, you are technically wearing the same cup size but the bra will fit better. It is this size confusion that causes women heartache, with some women having always worn a B cup they often don't want to hear that they should be wearing a D cup. Even if technically it is the same size, also what happens with some brands is that they don't offer the D cup option so women don't have the option to wear their correct size.

So, a 30F is equal to a 32E, 34DD, 36D, and 38C they are all the same cup size (See Fig 1). The next image shows a visual representation of this, showing women with the same breast capacity (cup size) but with different back sizes.

Unfortunately, standard cross grading cannot be used when it comes to larger cup sizes. Standard bra grading is un-dimensional, and takes no account of breast size, droop, shape, height, or width. Breasts over a certain cup size (and depending on the back size) have totally different shapes and drop etc. to the core size breast. This obviously also occurs with smaller breasts but the change is vaster in the bigger cup.
Also, when grading larger cup sizes, a standard grade can't be applied to each point. As the grade of the cup must be greater on the underarm side, so that the breasts still project forward.

Regarding wires when it comes to smaller sizes breasts (A, AA and AAA) although I'm yet to have designed directly for this section of the market, I'm led to believe the same wire which is a 30 is used throughout each size, so the width of the cup stays the same but the depth will be reduced in each size.

I asked Elma from Elma Lingerie an expert in designing and making lingerie for small cups, for more information on grading A cups bras.

"The depth will change, but the width can remain the same. You also should consider the positioning of the cups. AA/AAA cups will be set further apart (-0.5-1" gaps at the centre front) so the band must accommodate that as well."

www.elmashop.co

This could be why so many companies that start out supplying A-D cup size in lingerie and then expand to cover the larger sized cup market, often fail. They haven't considered the different grading needed to supply the larger cup market.

For example, if you applied the standard grade to a B cup and graded it up to an F cup, the apex of the bra would be too wide for the women's shoulders. With each grade for the larger cup market the apex would need to be moved in towards the centre of the body by a couple of mm with each grade, and in turn the other grades would have to accommodate for that.

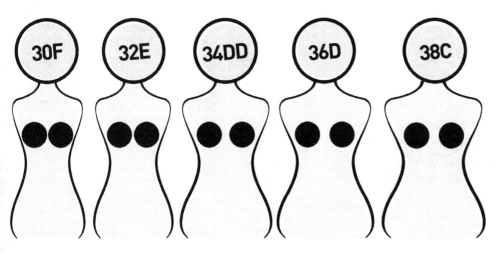

Fig 1

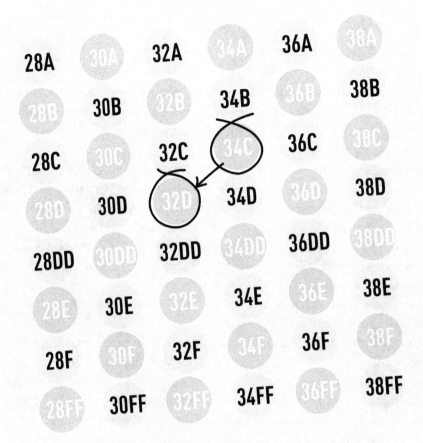

Still confused about cross grading?

The table above should also help make things clear; all the bra sizes diagonally are technically the same cup size. For example, a 28E, 30DD, 32D, 34C, 36B and 38A all have the same cup capacity.

If you are considering grading above a D cup, and starting out, I strongly recommend that you seek out a professional grader who understands and has knowledge on bra grading. When working above a D cup you are dealing with more volume and standard cross grading won't always work. Each new cup size should be taken as the base size for your next size up. When grading bras from a D cup to a DD cup, you will use the DD cup as your base size to grade to an E cup. It is important to get bra-grading right, for example if you're out 6mm that can mean you're into the next cup size.

GRADING A DARTED SOFT BRA

This darted soft bra has two pattern pieces to grade, a darted bra cup and a wing. A plus point is that as it's only one cup you have no seams (apart from the dart seams) to match up.

The only tricky part I think would be grading the dart seam, as you're grading the dart on a 45-degree angle. Like with the briefs we need to work out where the grade goes and in what direction and with what amount.

The grade cross lines will be as close in the middle of the pattern as possible and the whole pattern shall be graded (opposed to on the half with the brief). I would put the grade lines through points (corners) of the pattern, this is so when you shift a pattern, you can see that you are shifting it along the straight, it's easy to move it a couple of mm out, and this reference will make it easier.

Note that you may be shifting the pattern up, down left and right for one grade so four lines may have to be drawn either side of the guide lines.

Fig 1

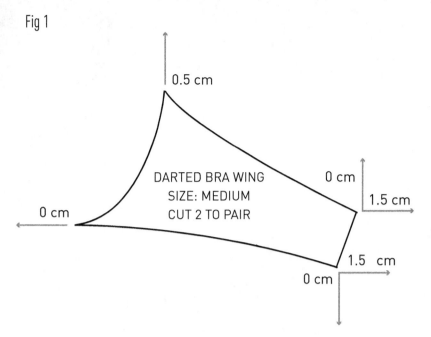

WHERE THE GRADE GOES SEE Fig 1

Let's start with the wing, you know from the previous measurements that the wing increases by 1.5cm and 'wing to cup' increases by 0.5cm. Starting at the top and moving in a clockwise direction as before, you will mark that the wing height will increase by 0.5cm – this is the 'wing to cup' measurement. (As the cup depth increases, so does the wing depth). The next point is the wing where the hook and eyes sit, all the increase will go on this point, so this will increase by 1.5cm (and the next point). No other points will grade.

SEE Fig 2

With the cups, you know that the depth and the width increases both by 1cm, so to split the grade evenly (top and bottom, left and right) each side of the pattern would increase by 0.5cm.

So, starting at the apex (top of the cup) each point would increase by 0.5cm, the next point (the underarm point) would increase by 0.5cm upwards and 0.5cm outwards. The darts need to grade in a diagonal line down and out by 0.5cm so the dart will follow the line, rather than just down otherwise the dart will become narrower.

Fig 2

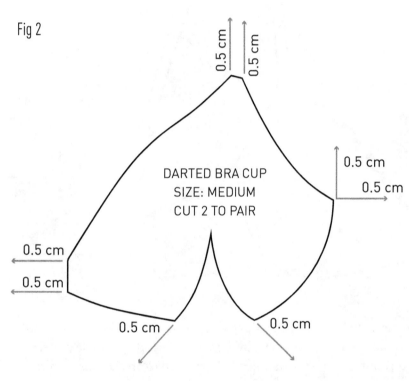

This grade can be done three ways:

_ Literally draw a 0.5cm line coming from that point (45-degree angle), then blend in the curve with the existing pattern. This is the way that will be used. This way is okay if you're not doing many sizes, and help you if you don't understand the other ways.

SEE Fig 3

_Turn the pattern a 45-degree angle each way, then re-draw in the guides, you would then move the pattern out by .5cm so in theory the pattern is always going across the 'X' axis.

_ Use the Pythagoras theory (only works in some angles of darts in that $a^2 \times b^2 = c^2$ as you shift across (a) and down (b) you've then got the length of c. So; to put it into numeric value $0.5^2 \times 0.5^2 = .6$

Due to the angle of the dart it ends up measuring 0.5cm after sewing.

Fig 3

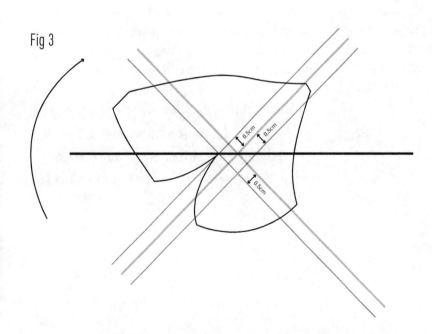

Fig 4

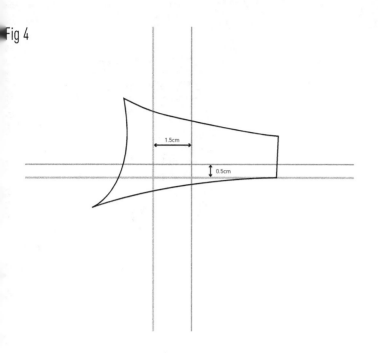

MARKING THE GRADE LINES SEE Fig 4

If we begin with the wing...
Staying with the same procedure of how you started the briefs, you draw around the pattern; mark the guides lines on the pattern (running vertically and horizontally) marking 0.5cm above the horizontal line and 1.5cm to the right of the vertical line.

SHIFTING THE PATTERN UP SEE Fig 5

First shift the pattern upwards by 0.5cm and mark in the new top of the pattern, then take the pattern to its original place then shift the pattern right 1.5cm and mark in the new place of the hooks and eye. The dark lines represent the new pattern line. SEE Fig 6

Fig 5

SHIFTING THE PATTERN UP. THE DARK LINE REPRESENTS THE NEW LINE.

Fig 7

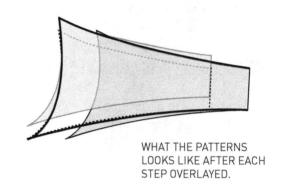

WHAT THE PATTERNS LOOKS LIKE AFTER EACH STEP OVERLAYED.

Figure 7 shows an overlap of the patterns at each stage, (the dotted line is the original pattern) and what the pattern would like at the end in the patterns were nested on top of one another.

Fig 6

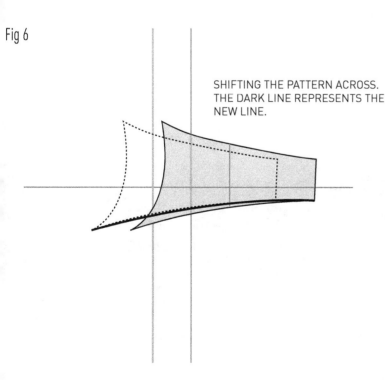

SHIFTING THE PATTERN ACROSS. THE DARK LINE REPRESENTS THE NEW LINE.

Fig 8

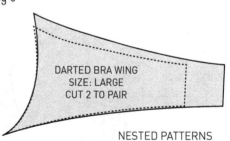

DARTED BRA WING
SIZE: LARGE
CUT 2 TO PAIR

NESTED PATTERNS

Figure 8 shows what they would look like if they were nested on top of one another.

CUPS

MARKING IN THE GRADE LINES   SEE Fig 9

Start with marking the guidelines and drawing the grade lines by the amount which you need to move the pattern by (left 5mm, right 5mm and up 5mm, leave the dart until last).

MOVING THE GRADE UP   SEE Fig 10

Move the cup up by 5mm and mark in the new top of the cup at the apex.

MOVING THE CUP UP AND TOWARDS CENTRE FRONT SEE Fig 11

Taking the pattern back to its original starting point, shift the pattern 5mm towards the Centre Front and mark in the new Centre Front.

MOVING THE CUP UP AND OUT   SEE Fig 12

Move the cup back to its original starting point and shift the pattern 5mm towards the side, and mark in your new pattern line.

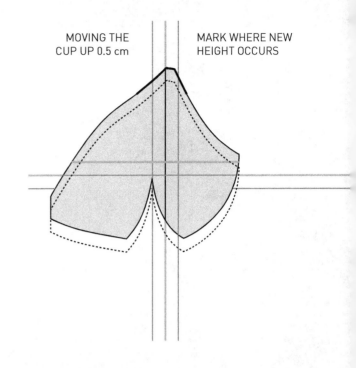

Fig 10

MOVING THE CUP UP 0.5 cm

MARK WHERE NEW HEIGHT OCCURS

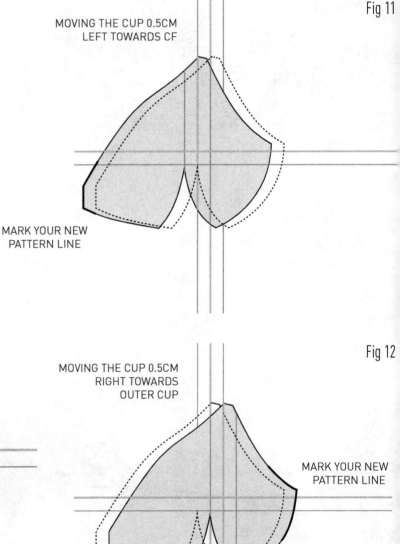

Fig 11

MOVING THE CUP 0.5CM LEFT TOWARDS CF

MARK YOUR NEW PATTERN LINE

Fig 12

MOVING THE CUP 0.5CM RIGHT TOWARDS OUTER CUP

MARK YOUR NEW PATTERN LINE

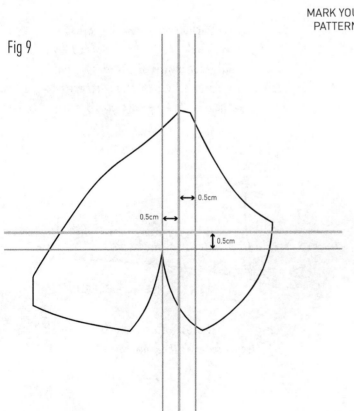

Fig 9

Fig 13

EXTENDING THE DART OUT BY 0.5CM

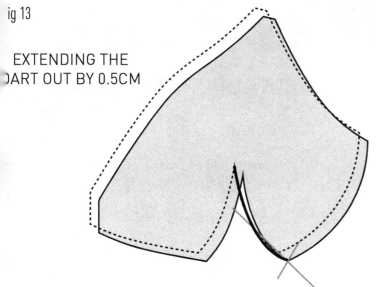

DARK LINE IS NEW DART LINE

EXTENDING THE DARTS OUT   SEE FIG 13

Draw a 45-degree angle from the point of the dart and mark 0.5cm along it, move the pattern piece to this point and mark in the new dart line. Repeat of other side of the dart.

DRAW 45 DEGREE ANGLE LINE OUT AND MARK 0.5CM DOWN THE LINE

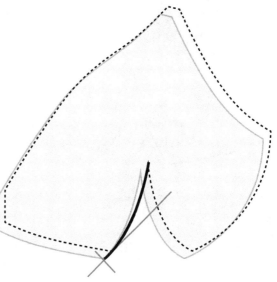

Fig 14

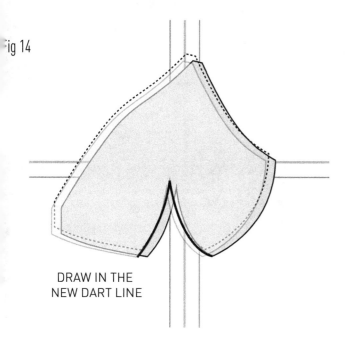

DRAW IN THE NEW DART LINE

DRAWING IN NEW DART LINES   SEE Fig 14

This shows all the pieces stacked up on each move that has been done, and the new dart lines drawn in.

ALL PATTERN MOVES STACKED   SEE Fig 15

All patterns stacked from each move and the new pattern piece traced off.

NESTED CUP PATTERNS CUP   SEE Fig 16

Both pattern pieces nested showing both sizes.

Fig 15

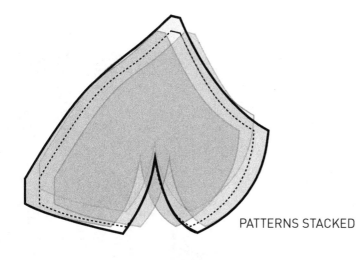

PATTERNS STACKED

Fig 16

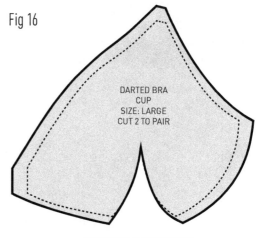

NESTED PATTERNS

Fig 17

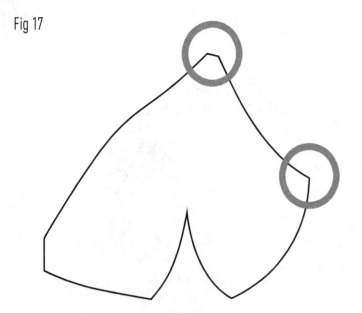

TROUBLESHOOTING WHEN GRADING

If you find that whilst grading the bra, that you are not getting the measurements you are needing to clear a grade size, then manually add the extra length at the two points highlighted. See Fig 17.

The reason you add on the outer part of the cup not the inner, is that by adding at the outer points you will then project the breast forward in its cup.

GRADING AN UNDERWIRE BRA

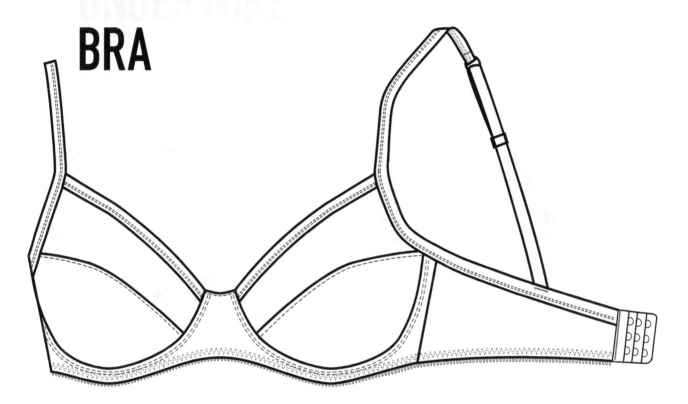

This underwire bra has a two-piece cup (upper and lower) and a full cradle (which means that the wing joins the centre front) so in total there are four pieces to be graded. You will be shown how to grade from a 34B to a 36B

So not only do you have to grade the cups but you must make sure they sit exactly within the cradle. As discussed the wire grade can be from 1.2 -2.1 or more depending on the wire type. Most wires will grade averagely by 1.5-2.1, so will be easier in practice.

As the wire is the most important if you're finding that the cup grades aren't fitting in and grading with the wire then alter them equally, i.e. if you must put extra grades (volume) on the cup make sure that the extra mm of the grade is split equally and 5mm (or however much) is not placed just on one point. I have graded this pattern by hand so you can see how it hand grades.

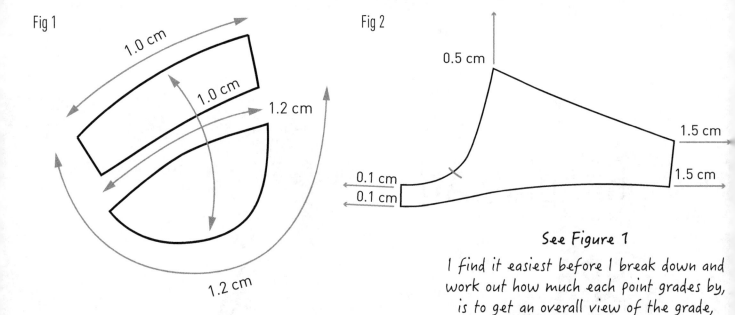

See Figure 1
I find it easiest before I break down and work out how much each point grades by, is to get an overall view of the grade, and how the cups grades to the cradle.

WHERE THE GRADE GOES SEE FIG 2

Let's start with the wing, you know from reading the measurements that the wing increases by 1.5cm and 'wing to cup' increases by 0.5cm. Starting at the top and moving in a clockwise direction as before, you will mark that the wing height will increase by 0.5cm (this is the 'wing to cup' measurement). As the cup depth increases, so does the wing depth.

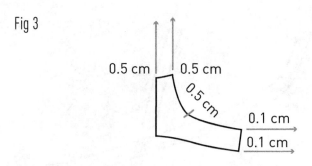

The next point is the wing where the hook and eyes sit, all the increase will go on this point, so this will increase by 1.5cm (and the next point). The point which sits under the cup will increase by 0.1cm (both points) so this means that along the curve it has increased approximately 0.6cm. You may have to play around with this point which is currently extending by 0.1cm, different shape curves will give you different increased measurements and may not grade as much as 6mm.The line crossing the pattern is a holding point which means that all the different size wings must stay at that point. This ensures that the curve stays the same throughout the grades.

If the wire graded by 1.6cm instead of 1.2cm then the 0.1cm grade would end up 0.3

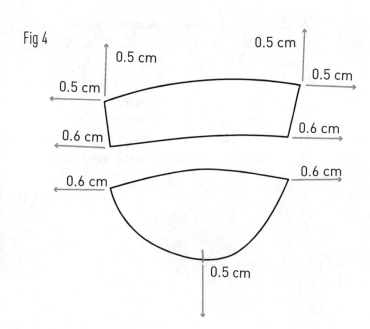

CENTRE FRONT   SEE Fig 3

Starting at the top points of the centre front (it's on the half) both points go up by 0.5cm, as a rule the CF (centre front) width never gets wider (unless you're doing specialist sizes). The next two points of the CF which join the wing go out by 0.1cm, this is total would then be 0.6cm (half of the 1.2cm that the cradle increases by). There is also a holding point on the CF which means that all the sizes will pass through this point so the curve doesn't get distorted. Remember that these measurements are only a starting point, if you're finding that the curve of your cradle isn't increasing by 0.6cm but only by 0.5cm, then you need to increase the 0.1cm to 0.2cm.

*If you must increase or decrease any of the measurements always go for the points which don't have a direct correlation with another piece. For example, when you look at the overview of the grade you note that the top of the cup increases by 0.5cm so it's easier to keep the top of the centre front doing the same.

CUPS   SEE Fig 4

Before you begin to grade the cups, I suggest putting them on the horizontal as you are grading up and down. If the cup sits at an angle shift the pattern so the bottom of the cup could sit along an imaginary ruler. The cups grade need to be split through both the top cup and bottom cup. The total width of the cup increases 1.2cm, the top of the cup increases 1.0cm, the depth of the cup is 1.0cm and the underwire increases by 1.2cm.

So, starting with the upper cup, looking at the grades you know the top cup width increases by 1.0cm, over the cup seam by 1.2cm and the depth by 0.5cm (half of the total grade of 1.0cm).

Starting at the top left, this point would shift up by 0.5cm and out by 0.5cm, and so would the next point. The next two points would go out by 0.6cm. The over the bust seam is extending by 0.2cm extra than the top of the cup, don't worry about this as this will allow the breast to project forward in the bigger sizes, and if you were to go above a D cup then you would adjust each cup grade accordingly.

*If this pattern were to be computer graded rather than hand graded then the 0.5cm would be split on the top line and bottom line so the top of the pattern and the bottom of the pattern would extend by 0.25cm, pretty much like when you drop a pebble into water all sides extend out.

As we are hand grading we are keeping it as simple as possible, so all the grade is going on the outer edge of the pattern, thereby keeping the over the bust seam as consistent as possible as that is the seam that will be sewn.

Starting at the left point on the lower cup this is extending out by 0.6cm matching the top cup point, the next point is also extended out by 0.6cm, so will be the total of 1.2cm.

The depth of the cup should increase by 0.5cm and as per the top cup all the grade is going on the outer side, as there is no point, you will mark one at the bottom. And it's this point that will drop down and increase by 0.5cm.

*Please note again the images for this grade will be hand graded, each point we grade will be shown by marking in the new grade then joining them up at the end.

WING

We begin grading the wing, by now you should know to trace around your pattern and draw vertical and horizontal guide lines both on the pattern you've traced around and on the new pattern that will become your larger pattern.

DRAWING IN GUIDELINES SEE Fig 5

On the newly traced pattern you will draw a line going horizontal 0.5cm above the original line and a vertical 1.5cm to the right of the vertical line, and 0.1cm to the left of the line.

SHIFTING THE PATTERN UP AND OUT SEE Fig 6

Move the pattern up 0.5cm and mark the top of the new pattern. Move the pattern back to its original position and shift the pattern 1.5cm to the right of the new drawn line; draw in the new pattern at the hook and eyes. Next move the pattern back to its original position then move it left 0.1cm and mark the new pattern increase at the lower of the wing.

JOINING UP ALL THE POINTS SEE Fig 7

Next using the pattern draw in the lines to blend in the new pattern to the old. The curve of the wing is just joined into original curve and the bottom of the pattern is blended into the bottom of the pattern.

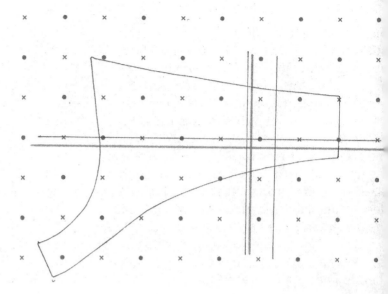

Fig 5

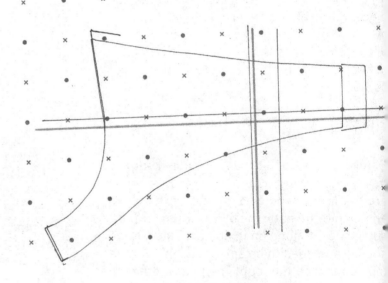

Fig 6

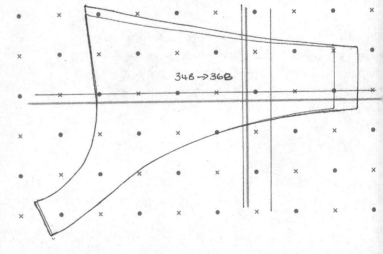

Fig 7

CENTRE FRONT

DRAWING IN THE GUIDELINES SEE Fig 8
After tracing the pattern and marking in your guidelines (new line horizontal 0.5cm above guide line and new line vertical 0.1cm to the right of the guide line).

SHIFTING THE PATTERN UP SEE Fig 9
Shift the pattern 0.5cm up and mark in the new top of the CF, return pattern to original point and shift it right 0.1cm and mark in new extended mark of the pattern.

JOINING THE LINES SEE FIG 10
When you've shifting the pattern up you'll note that the pattern has just been extended of its original size so no blending of the lines to the original pattern occurs

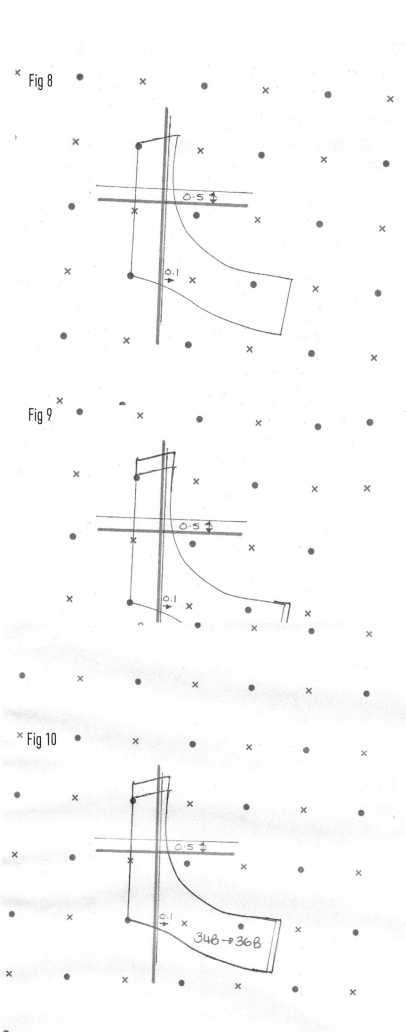

UPPER CUP

DRAWING IN THE GUIDELINES SEE Fig 11

Drawing around the pattern mark in the guidelines and grade lines (0.5cm horizontal above the guideline, and 0.5cm and 0.6cm vertical either side of the vertical guide line).

SHIFTING THE PATTERN SEE Fig 12

Shift the pattern up by 0.5cm and mark at the middle of the pattern the new height. Next shift the pattern 0.5cm left (with the pattern still shifted up) and mark the new position at the top, drawing around the corner of the pattern. Keeping the pattern shifted up, shift the pattern 0.5cm at the right of the vertical line and drawing around the corner of the apex point.

Take the pattern to the original position and shift the pattern 0.6cm to the left, and mark the bottom corner of the pattern. Next shift the pattern back and across to the right 0.6cm marking in the bottom corner of the pattern.

BLENDING THE LINES SEE Fig 13

With all the new markings, go around the pattern blending in each line with the next one.

Fig 11

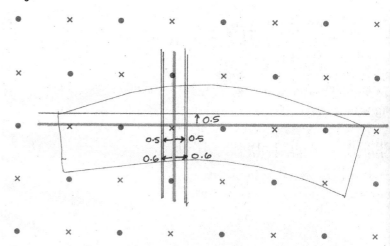

Fig 12

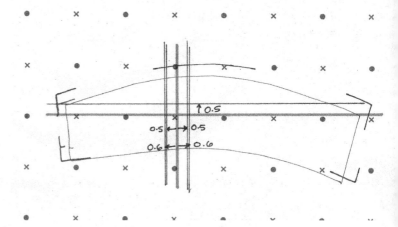

Fig 13

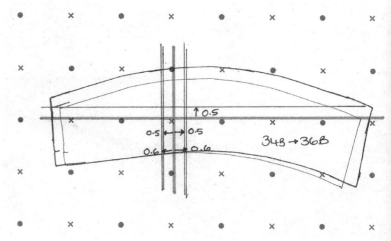

LOWER CUP

DRAWING IN THE GUIDELINES SEE Fig 14
Draw around the pattern and mark in the guidelines and grades lines (0.5cm horizontal line below the guideline, and 0.6cm vertical line either side of the guideline). I have marked a tiny line at 0.5 above the horizontal line to show that the cup at the centre point just shifts along the main guideline. This line can be helpful if you need to gauge if you've made a mistake and by how much if the pattern sits above the line, though it's not a necessary line.

SHIFTING THE PATTERN SEE Fig 15
Firstly, shift the pattern 0.6cm left and mark in the new point of the pattern, shift the pattern back and to the right 0.6cm marking in the new point. Bring the pattern back to the original position and shift the pattern down 0.5cm and mark in a new line for the pattern.

BLENDING IN THE LINE SEE Fig 16
Using the original pattern as a reference for the shape of the curve, join each new point together and blend in the new side points at the top of the pattern.

*Once graded take each pattern piece and walk along the sides of each pattern that will be sewn together (make sure each new pattern piece fits together).

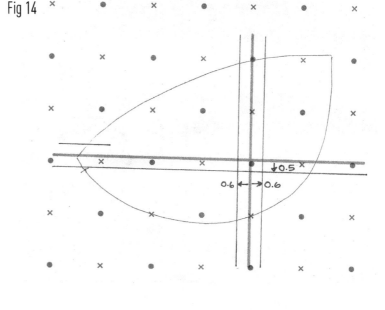

Fig 14

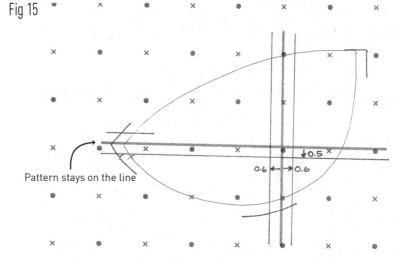

Fig 15

Pattern stays on the line

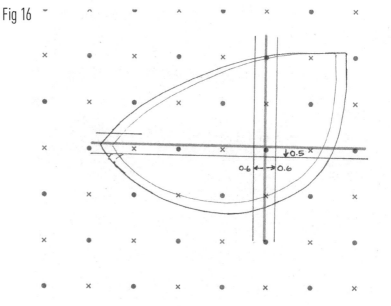

Fig 16

GRADING A ~~NON-WIRE~~ HIGH APEX BRA

This style of bra is a soft bra with a vertical seam on the cup and an under-band under the cup with a wing panel.

THE BEST WAY TO LEARN TO GRADE, IS TO GRADE!

So, this next grade of the bra I will talk you through the steps and you can then attempt to do it and check your result.

\ | | / /

I have hand graded this pattern and the results are at the back. Let's start with an overview of the pattern to see where the grade goes.

| | | | \

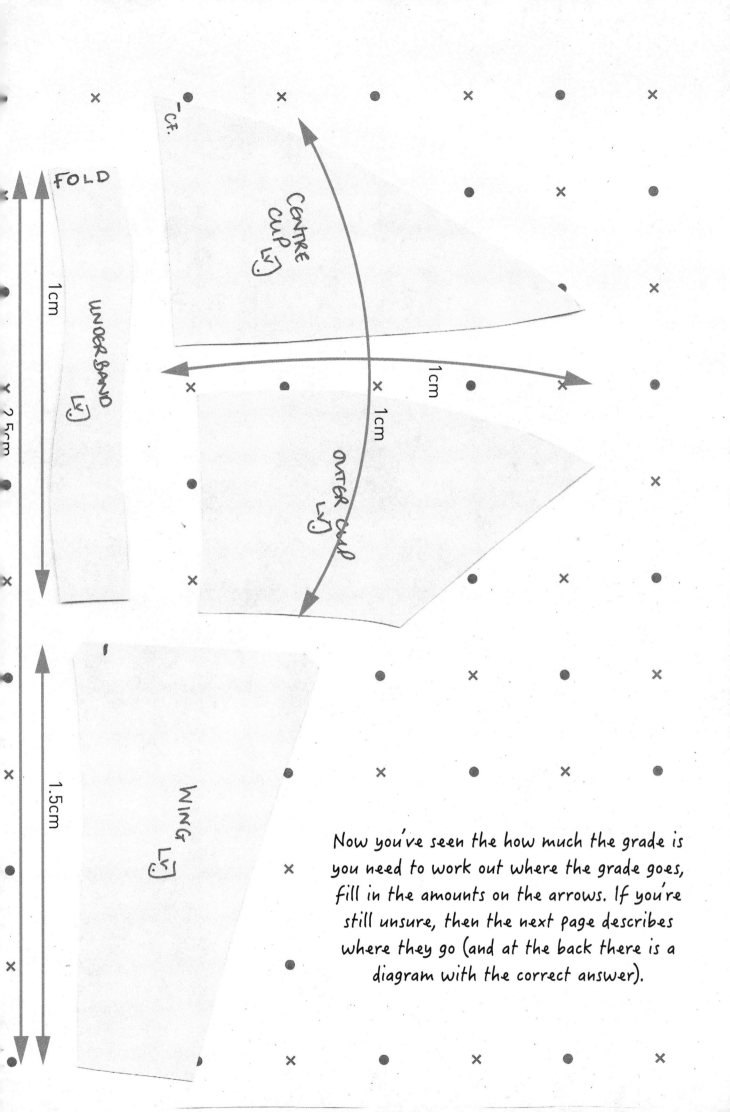

Now you've seen the how much the grade is you need to work out where the grade goes, fill in the amounts on the arrows. If you're still unsure, then the next page describes where they go (and at the back there is a diagram with the correct answer).

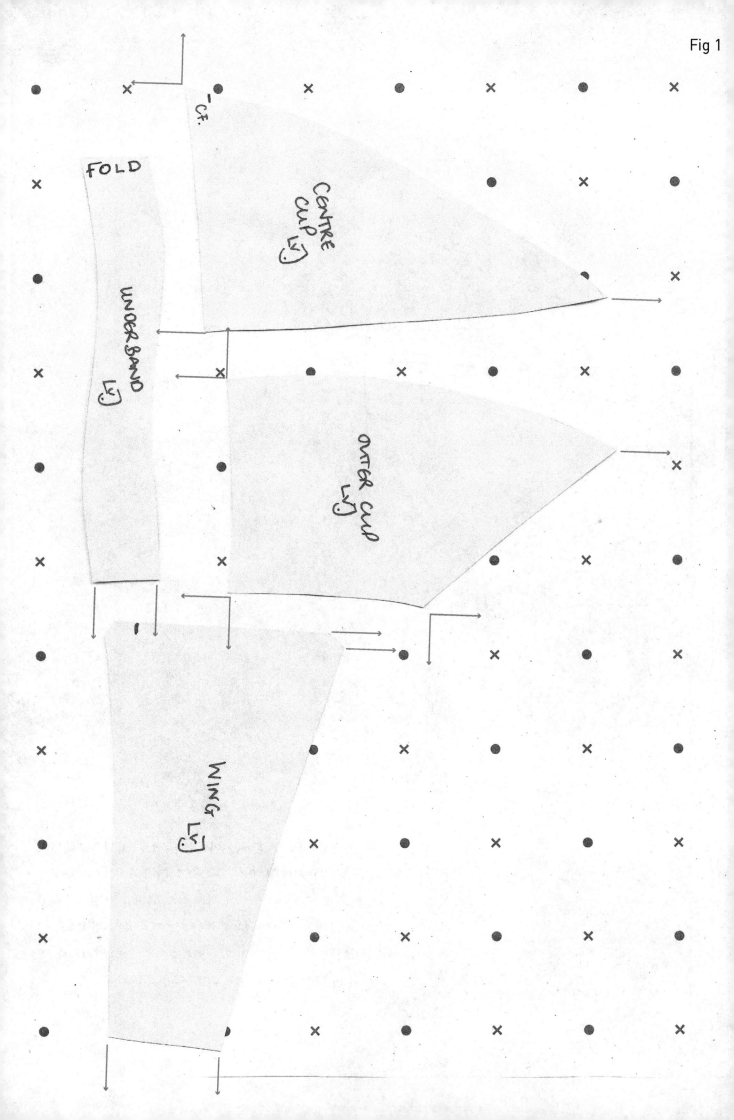

Fig 1

WHERE THE GRADE GOES SEE Fig 1

THE WING

Let's start with the wing, you know that the wing increases by 1.5cm and the wing height increases by 0.5cm. Starting at the top and moving in a clockwise direction as before, you will mark that the wing height will increase by 0.5cm – this is the 'wing to cup' measurement. (As the cup depth increases, so does the wing depth). There are two points at the top of the wing this is so when the pattern is sewn it considers the seam allowance and will sit flush against the cups.

The next points on the wing are where the hook and eyes sit, all the increase will go on these points, so these points will increase by 1.5cm. The wing where it meets the cup does not increase outwards.

UNDERBAND

This underband is on the half (the word FOLD is where it mirrors) so you will only need to grade one side. The height of the pattern doesn't increase only the width. The body fully around increases by 5cm per size so on the half it increases by 2.5cm. As the wing increase by 1.5cm you know that the cups and the underband width must increase by 1cm. So, at both side points the only grade to be applied is 1cm.

CENTRE CUP

The cup grades by 1cm horizontally and 1cm vertically. Like grading the underwire bra, all the grades will be going on the outer edge of the cup to keep the vertical seam curve consistent. Starting at the apex (the high point of the cup) this will grade 0.5cm upwards. The next point of the pattern (the bottom of the cup) will grade 0.5cm downwards, the next point (the centre front point) will grade 0.5cm to the left and 0.5cm downwards.

OUTER CUP

Starting at the apex (the highest point) in keeping with the previous grades of the centre cup, the point will grade 0.5cm upwards. Going in a clockwise manner the next point (underarm) the grade will be 0.5cm up and 0.5cm outwards. The next point (bottom of the cup) will grade 0.5cm outwards and 0.5cm downwards. The next point (centre seam) will grade 0.5cm downwards.

Now you are going to grade the patterns, you can either trace these or cut around them.
please note this pattern is not to scale.
And remember if you get stuck the results are at the back.

Fig 2

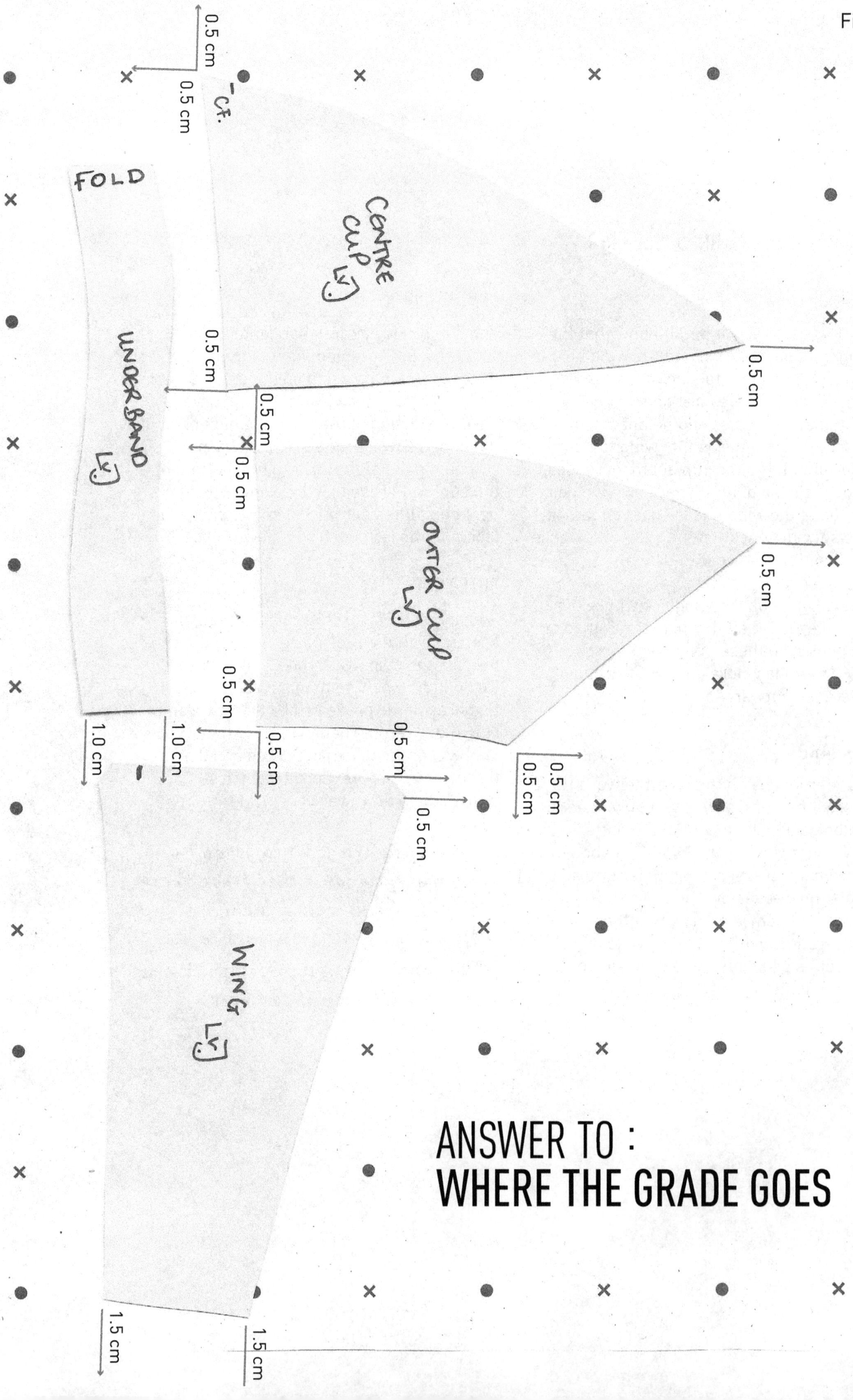

ANSWER TO: WHERE THE GRADE GOES

GRADING THE PATTERN SEE FOR THE RESULTS

WING

On the newly traced pattern draw in your cross shaped guidelines, then draw a line going horizontal 0.5cm above the original line and a vertical 1.5cm to the right of the vertical line. Move the pattern up 0.5cm and mark the top of the new pattern. Move the pattern back and shift the pattern 1.5cm to the right of the new drawn line and draw in the new line of the pattern at the hook and eyes Next using the pattern edge draw in line at the top of the pattern to join the newly raised pattern mark to the newly extended pattern.

UNDERBAND

After tracing around your pattern and marking in the guidelines (on both old and new pattern) draw a line 1.0cm vertical to the right of the guideline. Move the pattern 1.0cm to the right and mark around where the new pattern will be. Blend in the new pattern to the old.

CENTRE CUP

After drawing around the pattern and marking in the guidelines and grade lines (0.5cm horizontal above and below the guideline, and 0.5cm to the left of the vertical guide line). Shift the pattern up by 0.5cm and mark where the new apex will sit. Take the pattern to its original position and shift the pattern down 0.5cm, mark around where the new pattern will sit at the bottom. Keeping the pattern shifted down, shift the pattern to the left and mark around where the new pattern (at the centre front) will be.

Using the original pattern as template (draw around) join the new markings together to form the new pattern.

OUTER CUP

After drawing around the pattern and marking in the guidelines and grade lines (0.5cm horizontal above and below the guideline, and 0.5cm to the right of the vertical guide line). Shift the pattern up by 0.5cm and mark where the new apex will sit. Whilst the pattern is still shifted up, also shift the pattern 0.5cm to the right and mark around the next point (going clockwise) the underarm point. Take the pattern to its original position and shift the pattern down 0.5cm and out (right) and mark around the lower point (where the cup meets the wing). Take the pattern back to its original position and shift the pattern down 0.5cm and mark around the next point (going clockwise this will be the lower cup point where the two cups meet).

Using the original pattern as template (draw around) join the new markings to together to form the new pattern.

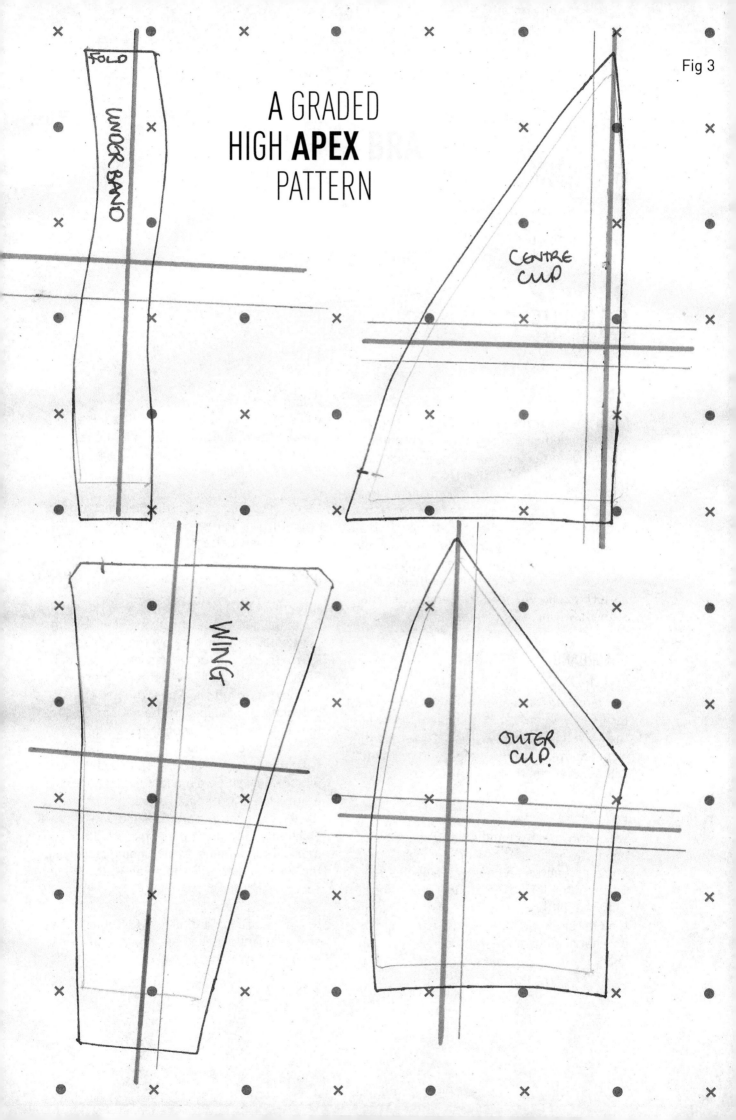
Fig 3

FINAL WORDS

You made it! Don't be put off if you've finished this book and your head is all over the place not quite understanding everything; this was the hardest (and longest time spent) writing this book so I know there is a lot to learn.

To understand how lingerie (especially the bra) grades and works, I recommend immersing yourself in trying different patterns and grading them. Go back over every part that you don't feel confident on draw out some lingerie shapes (they don't have to be real patterns at the start just shapes to get you started) and grade them. See what works and what you find hard.

When using real patterns, don't be scared to adjust the basic grades I have given you, especially if you are working with woven fabrics.

Great lingerie is lingerie that fits you well and makes you feel comfortable and confident when wearing it. Would you trust a mechanic to fix your car who didn't know the parts or how they work?

You must marry the logical side of adding in measurements to the aesthetics of making a garment look beautiful.

The hardest part of working out grading is always the beginning. A contact page can be found at www.vanjonssondesign.com if you have any further questions. I will answer the best I can and if I don't have the right answers I will direct you to where you can find them. There is also a blog in which you can follow, which is updated with tips, advice and how-to's about Lingerie.

ABOUT THE AUTHOR

Laurie van Jonsson started out with an obsession for lingerie that she just couldn't cure. With her infatuation for all things beautiful, she graduated from De-Montfort University and became a Lingerie and Swimwear designer for a UK manufacturer designing for the UK high street stores. Wanting to see the world, van Jonsson bought a one-way ticket to Thailand and whilst there secured work designing swimwear. Upon returning to the UK, with her fascination with finding the perfect fitting bra van Jonsson launched her own lingerie label – Vanjo, a brand that catered for small backs and bigger cup sizes.

"I believe that all things should be designed with intent and not just look appealing to the eye but that this should be a bi product of good design."

It was whilst running Vanjo; that the idea of writing "How to become a Lingerie Designer" came about; van Jonsson would receive requests from people about how to launch their own lingerie label or want advice about how to do costs or specification sheets. Becoming a freelance designer allowed her the time to complete her two passions, writing and designing. It also led her to work internationally from Ireland to Australia. With the success of the first book, van Jonsson now writes and designs full time, and ha relaunched Vanjo.

BOOKS FROM SAME AUTHOR

HOW TO BECOME A LINGERIE DESIGNER

THE ANATOMY OF THE BRA

HOW TO SPEC A BRA & BRIEF

HOW TO WRITE A BRA & BRIEF TECH PACK

REFERENCES

Websites

https://www.clothingpatterns101.com/pattern-grading.html
https://www.craftsy.com/sewing/article/easy-guide-pattern-grading/
http://textilelearner.blogspot.com/2014/03/methods-of-garment-pattern-grading.html
https://en.wikipedia.org/wiki/Pattern_grading

Magazines

Sew it Vintage
The Threads Magazine

CPSIA information can be obtained
at www.ICGtesting.com
Printed in the USA
BVHW011234181119
563835BV00017B/177/P